LANGUAGE PARASITES

Before you start to read this book, take this moment to think about making a donation to punctum books, an independent non-profit press

@ https://punctumbooks.com/support

If you're reading the e-book, you can click on the image below to go directly to our donations site. Any amount, no matter the size, is appreciated and will help us to keep our ship of fools afloat. Contributions from dedicated readers will also help us to keep our commons open and to cultivate new work that can't find a welcoming port elsewhere. Our adventure is not possible without your support.
Vive la open-access.

Fig. 1. Hieronymus Bosch, *Ship of Fools* (1490–1500)

First published in 2017 by punctum books, Earth, Milky Way.
https://punctumbooks.com

ISBN-13: 978-0-9985318-6-1
ISBN-10: 0-9985318-6-3
Library of Congress Cataloging Data is available from the Library of Congress

Book design: Vincent W.J. van Gerven Oei
Cover image: Sean Braune and Michael F Bergmann, *Foams,* acrylic on canvas,
2017. Photo by Michael F Bergmann.

SEAN BRAUNE

LANGUAGE PARASITES

Of Phorontology

Table of Contents

Phorontology

P HORONTOLOGY IS THE ONTOLOGICAL STUDY of an inter-
mediary category of sites. The biological doctrine of *phoresis* is the practice of parasitic migration upon a larger
organism. A *phoront* is a specific category of symbionts that
travel upon larger organisms and engage in phoresis or migration. The sloth moths **Bradipodicola hahneli** and **Cryptoses
choloepi** are two types of phoronts that live in the fur of sloths
and use them for travel. A phoront lives upon a larger creature
and, like a vagrant or menacing hitchhiker, does not pay for gas.

In the contemporary world, issues of phoresis are omnipresent, 'pataphysically traceable to the Aristotelian tradition of
phronesis. Such wordplay reveals an underlying relationship between parasitic correlationism and practical wisdom. Phronesis
is an epistemological mode that judges the world according to
its own internal laws. When translated into Latin as *pruden-
tia* — the term from which jurisprudence derives — an indeci-
pherable knot is produced between the legal and the biological. Emerging from philosophy as practical wisdom, phronesis
evokes a particular *Weltanschauung* that apprehends the world
as arguably parasitic. Contemporary phronesis should be related to phoresis because it is only through understanding parasitic migration that a radical theorization of subjects, objects, and
transjects can occur. Phorontology situates and sites these various entities as components of a larger being called a *xenoject,*
which is a subjective entity thrown very far afield from "normative" Deleuzo-Foucauldian folds or Lacano-Freudian knots.

Phronesis, in phorontology, when combined with phoresis,
situates an underlying structural model of the world in which
every traditional human subject becomes nothing but a glo-

rified phoront riding on the back of a larger creature. In "On Truth and Lies in a Nonmoral Sense," Nietzsche writes: "Here one may certainly admire man as a mighty genius of construction, who succeeds in piling up an infinitely complicated dome of concepts upon an unstable foundation, and, as it were, on running water."[1] When conceived of as a phoront (or as being composed of phoronts), the draconian human subject is relegated to a thing that is cast adrift in the Heraclitean river — never fixed, never stable — where, caught in the fluctuations of water, any sense of being becomes strange and alien. The subject is dead and the xenoject and the transject emerge. These new *jects* are thrown from Zarathustra's mountain and walk — protean and parasitic — down to the marketplace or the shopping mall. And where are these new jects headed? To dinner of course!

Sites and Constructions

Sites are spaces. A site is non-coded and exists apart from correlational reality, remaining anterior to apprehensions of language, meaning, or system. A site is a space upon which things are *built* and a building is then a place that, whether constructed or deconstructed, has a particular shape, appearance, or representation.

Nothing is built, in phorontology, *ab nihilo* in that traditional construction projects require a superstitious ritual that sanctifies the ground. A cornerstone is the term for a sanctified object that designates the land as safe for construction. In Europe, until the early twentieth century, cornerstones were locations of sacrifice: cats, dogs, and even women were ritually slaughtered in the service of cornerstones in order to purify the land and permit a reliable construction. To this day, the ritual holds true — albeit in a less barbarous manner — when a coin or a time capsule is placed in the ground prior to the construction of

---

1   Friedrich Nietzsche, "On Truth and Lies in a Nonmoral Sense," *Philosophy and Truth: Selections from Nietzsche's Notebooks of the Early 1870s,* ed. and trans. Daniel Breazeale, 79–91 (New Jersey: Humanities Press, 1979), 85.

a tall office tower. Humans appear to require the sanctification of construction projects.

A good textual example of the tradition of the corner-stone can be found in the iconic Romanian text "Monastirea Argeşului" — an anonymous oral ballad handed down from generation to generation. The poem features Meşterul Manole (or "Master Manole"), a master architect charged with building Prince Negru Voda's new monastery. In order to sanctify the building project, Manole and his men build the walls around the living body of his wife, Ana (who is pregnant with their child). The sacrifice of Ana and her baby permits the construction of the monastery. The poem is obviously misogynistic and epitomizes the tradition of the cornerstone in that, in patriarchal culture, every foundation requires some form of oblation or sacrifice. A previous construction anticipates future constructions in an unfolding seriality of architectural and architextual emergence. Nothing can be constructed *ab nihilo* because every construction requires an originary parasite that can *site* the future building as a site that is not of the site. The hidden parasite is foundational when ontology becomes *phorontology*.

A place, once built, presents as an image or appearance that has a specific emergence in temporality. As a place, this image instates subsequent events, occasions, experiences, and *situations*. A situation is a meeting place or gathering of subjects, objects, abjects, projects, dejects, and rejects. A situation is an event constituted by a variety of parasites that remain hidden within the instated specificity of gridlines. These parasites self-organize in an overall system that develops according to rules of emergence. What I call "the site" is meant to describe an ontological space of fractal emergence so that, in other words, the site permits the concrescence of a seriality of construction sites. The site enables systems of meaning, sense, and substance to emerge alongside the fantasmatic and the imaginary.

Phorontology approaches these strange entities via an alternative or anterior pathway that can be located at a *Res-in-situ* — at a situated or sited Thing. There are no "coherent" subjects or objects that can be found in a phorontological perspective because both standardized categories (as "subject" or "object") are only existent when sited or situated. Abjects and rejects, objects and dejects all similarly manifest within situations. A site, being initially un-coded, becomes re-coded as a Res-in-situ when a thing is positioned in relation to a corresponding intersection point of codes and meaning-productions. The thing is sited here in and as a place where situations and occasions can and do occur. However, the sited thing — whether subject, object, project, deject, reject, or abject — is consistently focalized as a para-site in relation to a larger process of sites and situating-spaces.

Ontological and metaphysical inquiry should not focus on either the subject or the object or any hermeneutic that *privileges* an entity or thing that has been "thrown"; instead, ontology and metaphysics should proceed by way of a phorontology, which I conceive as a program that studies the ontological status of sites and parasites. In *Microcosmos* (1986), Lynn Margulis and Dorion Sagan claim that "[t]he reality and recurrence of symbiosis in evolution suggests that we are still in an invasive, 'parasitic' stage and we must slow down, share, and reunite ourselves with other beings if we are to achieve evolutionary longevity."[2]

The Copernican Revolution (found in both Copernicus for astronomy and Kant for philosophy) situates a revolution of consciousness — a spitting in the face of acceptable opinion. A pinion, the same one that resides within machines, eventually develops into an *I-pinion* of proliferating cycles, differences, and repetitions (alongside their different-repetitions and repetitive-differences). The I-pinion turns, revolves, evolves, and involves the whole corpus of the machine in the minutiae of its independent parts. The part is apart and a part from the whole, but the whole is a part and apart of the part. This perhaps frustrating phrasing presents one of the most important contributions of fractal geometry to anthropocentric knowledge-systems in that

---

2 Lynn Margulis and Dorion Sagan, *Microcosmos: Four Billion Years of Evolution from Our Microbial Ancestors* (Berkeley: University of California Press, 1997), 196.

there remains — in natural shapes and objects — an ontological resistance to the firm differentiation between an apparent macrocosmos and an apparent microcosmos.

This book re-imagines the parasite of Michel Serres from the perspective of the site itself, which is the site that the parasite occupies. The term "parasite" derives, etymologically, from *parasitus* (Latin) and *parasitos* (Greek), meaning "a person who eats at the table of another." It can mean "feeding beside," from *para* (beside) and *sitos* (wheat, flour, bread, or food). The scientific definition of a parasite as an animal or plant that lives on or inside others emerges in 1646, but the original definition denotes the sycophantic or Machiavellian implication of a "hanger-on" (from 1539 onwards). Arguably, the 1539 definition is the dominant (but not exclusive) meaning used by Serres; however, in *Language Parasites,* I argue that a parasite is something else as well: the parasite is also a *para-site*. In other words, there is a site that can be found beside the original — a site that contains the meaning of the original as simulation or fractal.[3] This *para* can be considered the epiphenomenon of the phenomenon, and, as such, manifests as the unconsidered supplement that is negated by anthropocentric and epistemological systems of segmentation.

A way of grounding or siting a phorontological theory is to consider *real parasite-bodies* and ask: *what is the Being of a parasite or the parasites?* The question that extends from this initial query is: *what are the constructions or segmentations that allow and are allowed by such a notion of Being?* For example, the male sheep crab Loxorhynchus grandis is commonly infected by a parasitic barnacle called Heterosaccus californicus and the crab becomes female: its abdomen widens and the parasitic infection creates a womb in the crab. The male sheep crab's entire ontology changes, but its ontology is never strictly "in-itself" because the transformation requires the inclusion or assistance of a parasitic other that is also a *parasitic self.* The Other, in the instance of phorontology, is often on the inside and acts as a

---

3   Benoit B. Mandelbrot, *The Fractal Geometry of Nature* (New York: W.H. Freeman and Company, 2000).

belonging-self that constructs a metamorphic-inside or the very possibility of an inside. The logic of the parasite is not theoretical, abstract, or obscure, but real: the parasite induces and produces *real processes* of metamorphosis. Following this line of reasoning, the most frightening aspect of Franz Kafka's *The Metamorphosis* (1915) is not that Gregor Samsa awakens as a large bug, but rather, that the parasite responsible for Samsa's transformation is never found. The genus of the originary parasite is never identified or taxonomically clarified in Kafka's text. In this sense, Kafka's writing can be considered an evocation or clinical diagnosis of a particular kind of originary parasite: *the parasite of the modern and contemporary subjective condition.*

The white butterfly wasp Cotesia glomerata infects the cabbage butterfly Pieris brassicae. The process begins when the cabbage butterfly, as a caterpillar, protects the wasp larvae below its body after the parasites have burrowed out of the caterpillar's abdomen in order to spin their cocoon. *Language Parasites* primarily focuses on male writers and thinkers — the reason for this may be immediately apparent because, historically speaking, "man" and men have occupied parasitic positions in both patriarchy and colonialism. As well, like any parasitic process, epistemology and philosophy develop from a variety of parasitic traditions. My subtitle, *Of Phorontology,* echoes Derrida's *Of Grammatology* (1967), but it is its own entity while at the same time feeding off of Derrida's original. Philosophy is parasitical. The purpose of this work is to suggest a new system that I term "phorontology," which is a system or program that can be used to engage or interrogate the para-sites that extend beside and beyond their originary sites. I consider phorontology to be "the study of sites, para-sites, and parasitic being."

However, the sites that I engage with cannot be approached at their origin; therefore, they are entered through their para-sites. As I mentioned earlier, *sitos* in Greek originally means "food." Fittingly, food is not simply connotative of food itself, but also of the normative ideologies that surround consumption and commensality. The parasite de-consumes through its consummation. The notion of the *sitos* is concerned with food, eating, mastication, digestion, belching, and shitting — the whole of the human anatomy is at work in the concept of *sitos* — and the whole of human society is at work also, with its cycles of negentropy and entropy or reversal and redemption. Humans enjoy eating in groups that ritualize the consumption of food — we fetishize chewing, eating, and feeding. The restaurant and the grocery store are economic assemblages that will never go out of business because **Homo sapiens** are social by virtue of the ritualization, temporalization, and spatialization of the intake of food. We know where we are because we eat within specific locales. Serres is quite right when he points out our parasitical social order, but the subtlety found in the *para-site* can be considered in the emphasis placed on the *sitos*. It is difficult to contend that civilization would have "caught on" if it were not for the social rituals that surround eating and the related structures of etiquette.

The *sitos* of phorontology connotes not only food, but also mastication and digestion — it is fully anatomical and fully *automatic* — we eat, we socialize as we chew, and we digest without thinking too much about it. The parasitic flatworm **Ribeiroia ondatrae** infects the American bullfrog **Lithobates catesbeianus** and inspires the growth of extra legs so that the bullfrog is easy prey for herons. The herons that eat the bullfrog are also consuming the flatworm's eggs, which are then released through the heron's feces. The most interesting aspects of human society are the parts that we do not think about. The *parts* of society are, in this sense, anatomical and automatic. They are anatomic (in parts), automatic in how they function, and atomic (as a whole). The parts of society work in relation — in diffracted and diffracting networks. Phorontology analyzes that which *is not considered*; or, put differently, phorontology is "food" for the mind that simultaneously *eats the mind*. Phorontology consumes philosophy, authors, and readers because the parasite(s) wait over phorontology's shoulder. The parasite is, conceptually speaking, the realist manifestation of an unconsidered shadow or supplement. The parasite is a swerve or an N — it is unknown. It is simultaneously that which gnaws at the base of consciousness and also consciousness itself.

Is the site ever the *subject*? Perhaps, but the site can just as easily be *voided* or *avoided*. This "void" is formed and informed by the relation of the para-site to the para-site or by the chain of para-sites that live or manifest *beside* the para-site, thereby creating a chain of fractal sites *ad infinitum*. The amphipod Hyalella azteca is invaded by Pseudocorynosoma constrictum (a parasitic worm that can only grow in the digestive tracks of birds) and the worm reprograms the amphipod's brain so that it will swim up to the water's surface and be eaten by birds. Pattern recognition and the metamorphoses of patterns: patterns are repetitively re-cognized to reinstate the same. Ideologies do sometimes change, but perhaps the patterns do not. This situation describes why the revolution will not arrive.

Occasionally, the ideology of science changes, but this change becomes incorporated into a pattern of sameness or repetition. The awareness of the parasite permits a Copernican shift in the ontology of the subject because the subject transforms — according to the program of the parasite — initially to the postmodern and then later to the posthuman. To understand this transformation, we have to understand the localities and diffracting beings of the *site* and the *para-site*. This development is not the result of a type of reaction formation, but rather of the *parasite of constraint* that influences, infects, and feeds side-by-side with the *hôte*.

The concept of the "parasite of constraint" will be returned to throughout *Language Parasites*. The parasite of constraint is both a guest and a host and it is living inside you and with you (dear reader, dear scholar, dear thinker). Sometimes, it speaks for you. Sometimes, it listens. At other times, it influences, decides, and formulates as its thoughts and impressions are inextricable from your own. *It thinks* and *it speaks*; or, I speak and I think. This chiasmus formulates the relation between the site and the para-site because language is produced from an *other* site — from an "elsewhere." The parasite of constraint is, in this sense, language. The parasite of constraint writes and speaks.

It teaches us through the discipline of epistemology and the institutional systems of academia and media. Maybe there *is* a spiraling tapeworm wrapped tightly around the "insides" of knowledge and discourse.

But isn't this assertion similar to saying that "every message is ideological?" In some ways, certainly; however, the behavior patterns of the parasite of constraint suggest that the logic of the ideological points *not* to an internal logic or to an internal *illogic*, but rather, to an interior *illness*. An ideological message is typically tainted in some way and this "off-kilter" quality that is omnipresent in the ideological leaves us susceptible to parasitic infection. The parasite of constraint is not necessarily air-borne because it infects through the realms of the *visual,* the *auditory,* and the *spoken*. This parasite is born inside all of us as extra ribs. The tangibility of the object called the "brain" is already parasitical: it is a bumpy, curly, and unknown mass that "exists" inside our skull. The parasite of constraint is intrinsic to language and culture and can be focalized in the *subjective site* as a *Res-in-situ.*

Even if we have historically moved into (and out of) the postmodern, then we still stand at the corpus's feet, hypnotized by what I call *postmortemism*. The corpus is dead and has become a corpse after the parasite has hollowed out its insides. We have historically moved beyond the posthuman and begun its dissection. The spark of "newness" or "nowness" has long since been evacuated by the sense of cold flesh on the cold steel of the autopsy table. Torpor and rigidity have set in and the sentience of the parasites is all that is left. I would go further: we are living in an era of *metasentient parasites.*

I will eat French theory and its leftovers. I will become a parasite of thought. Why? Because every thought is already a parasite. Philosophy is filled with Hegel-parasites, Derrida-parasites, Cixous-parasites, Serres-parasites, Harman-parasites, Kristeva-parasites, Laruelle-parasites, de Beauvoir-parasites, and countless other parasites. There is no escape from the parasites of thought. At the very least, every "is" and every declarative sentence in *Language Parasites* is a material parasite; or, in other words, this book is the result of a *continental philosophical infection.*

What is called "the subject" is subject *of* various constraints. If society is situated as a site, then the subject becomes a para-site. Linguistic and logical feedback can be found everywhere. This feedback can be found in even the most banal communication. Linguistic feedback is supplemental to normative communication and hints at a kind of semantic void that watches over the subject's shoulder. This loop is chaotic and fractal and repeats itself forever — as a stammering in echoes, without solution.

Phorontology considers the fundamental arbitrariness of sites. Phorontology offers a new approach to theories of Being because before Being can be addressed, there must be a site that situates being *as Being* or existence as an existence that exists. Prior to the deconstruction of a philosophical edifice or artifice, there must have been a site for the original philosophy-forma-tion — a construction site for philosophy. Why was an artifice built *here* and not *there*? Or, why was a philosophy built in *this* way and not a *different* way? These questions are phorontologi-cal. Why consider Being at all when the related considerations of parasite places and spaces or parasite temporalities have yet to be addressed? Phorontology considers the fractal origins of philosophy. Fractals are bumpy, fuzzy, and folded geometrical formations and parasites love hiding in folds and furrows. How can we investigate existence without first considering the site(s) that yield(s) existence?

Have we moved beyond the historical? If we have, then perhaps we have entered into a phase that could be called *hyper-history*. We should remember Giambattista Vico's conception of history in the *Scienza Nuova* (1744): his concept of *storia ideale eterna* or *ideal eternal history* is summarized in his concept of the *ricorso*. The *ricorso* considers an eternal model of history that recurs through three essential ages: the ages of Gods, Heroes, and Man. This early structural model of history is parasitic because of its intrinsic recursivity: Vico's "epochs" recur as historical fractals that likewise fold into the fractality of the subject and the other subjects of history. The picture here becomes one of feedback upon feedback upon feedback. Recursive history is a hyperhistory of pure forward momentum — an accelerationist nightmare. We are moving too fast, but it should be noted that, from a phorontological perspective, history (like consciousness) is *metafractalic.*

Of course, by using the term "hyperhistory" I am building on Baudrillard's use of the term "hyperreal."[4] The hyperreal denotes the simulation of the real as a site that grounds the real, but without origin. The hyperreal sites an epistemic shift in the real, but any shift in the real must accompany a contingent shift in the historical. "Hyperhistory" designates a notion of world history that is no longer cumulative, but constellated. What I call "hyperhistory" coincides with the accelerated sense of time that corresponds to the emergence of contemporary industry, technology, and specifically the rise of the Internet. The Internet permits everyone with a cable connection to create her or his own personal history everyday. For this reason, there is no longer *one history,* but rather, multiple histories. Certainly, one way of thinking about the hyperhistorical is to invoke the Deleuzoguattarian concept of the rhizome because hyperhistory has no origin, linearity, or definable boundary. Another way to think of hyperhistory is to consider the recent interest in the concept of accelerationism made popular in the Nick Srnicek and Alex Williams manifesto written in 2013.[5]

However, beyond other possible conceptual allegiances, hyperhistory is phorontological. Why? Because even though the site is arbitrary, fractal, and indefinite, it remains *a site.* Despite the multiplication of possibilities and the relativization of subjectivities, histories will of necessity be "killed off" to permit the full autocratic reign of hyperhistory. However, it should be mentioned that the hyperhistorical is impossible if the contemporary representation of the subject were not metafractalic. The

---

4   Jean Baudrillard, *Simulacra and Simulation,* trans. Sheila Faria Glaser (Ann Arbor: University of Michigan Press, 1994), 22–23.
5   Alex Williams and Nick Srnicek, "#Accelerate: Manifesto for an Accelerationist Politics," *#ACCELERATE: The Accelerationist Reader* (Falmouth: Urbanomic, 2014), 347–62.

ontology of the subject is *self-similar* to the "ontology" of the historical. For this reason, the metafractality of the subject extends into the metafractality of history.

The Latin proverb rings true here: *Nomen est numen* or "to name is to know." We have a lot of concepts in philosophy and theory: concepts such as the "absolute," the "transcendent," "noumena," "phenomena," "ego," "id," "unconscious," "line of flight," "heteroglossia," "rhizome," "*sinthome,*" "*objet petit a,*" "*différance,*" etc. I consider each of these concepts to be both discoveries and inventions. The unconscious has become real whether we agree with the concept or not. The quantum world has become real even though we have no hope of ever "seeing" it. The rhizome is real when we look at or think about interlocking structures of visceral or virtual complexity. Sometimes reality exists and sometimes "reality" does not exist. It certainly depends. *Nomen est numen.* To name means to nominate or carve out a place in history and epistemology and this humanist or posthumanist mode of nomination permits the creation of what I call a de-scission.[6] In other words, every concept is *cut* — sometimes forcefully and sometimes elegantly — out of the cloth of necessity and contingency. If the subject is experiencing a parasitic infection — an infection that lurks at the depths of its language and ontology — then we need *new* concepts that can begin to fend off the invasion.

Hyperhistory is also *spectaclysmic.* In the rapid speed of our accelerated history, traditional notions of history have been replaced by the infinite histories that are propagated by modern technologies. History is now too big to read or to know and there is too much of it. History is now hyperhistorical: it does not have linearity or "plot progression" and its cast of characters is far larger than anything that can ever be conceived. There is no longer any possibility of "historical narrative." History, prior to its own death, has imposed sites onto the landscape. "His-

---

6   My concept of "de-scission" is related to Ray Brassier's choice to translate Heidegger's *Unter-schied* as "de-scission." See Ray Brassier, *Nihil Unbound: Enlightenment and Extinction* (London: Palgrave Macmillan, 2007), 131.

torical sites" they are called or "heritage homes": consider the scene in Don DeLillo's *White Noise* (1985) when Jack Gladney and Murray Jay Siskind visit the "Most Photographed Barn in America" — the barn is only notable because it is marketed as "the most photographed barn." The site is therefore a pure construction. Siskind recognizes that there is nothing intrinsic about this particular barn that makes it notable beyond its symbolic and cultural cache.

The sites keep changing. The horsehair worm **Paragordius varius** and the house cricket **Acheta domesticus** are locked in a relationship of parasite and host: the horsehair worm uses the cricket as a host, eventually inducing the cricket to commit suicide by diving into a body of water and drowning so that the mature horsehair worm (sometimes measuring a foot long) can swim to its future. Like the horsehair worm, every major intellectual tradition in human history situates itself in relation to a specific site: relativism, phenomenology, existentialism, deconstruction, psychoanalysis, scientism, sociology, anthropology, psychology, structuralism, constructivism, positivism, nihilism, metaphysics, Marxism, fascism, 'Pataphysics, situationism, surrealism, Dadaism, impressionism, etc., each exist as the discursive productions of an antagonism against an immanent construction. Each discourse emerges here as a response — as a para-site to a site.

Every site and every situation is dialogistic in that they allow for responses, but these responses do not exist as infinities, but as finite continua. These continua inaugurate counter-sites or para-sites that are responsive, but these para-sites can themselves become sites when an ideologically "new" discourse implants inside them and grows like an embryogenetic building. *Why this one site and not another?* Notions such as "discourse," "hegemony," "ideology," and "mythology" each require a site to ground them. *Grund.* What allows one site to develop a dominant thought-episteme instead of another? These are phorontological questions. Phorontology, now as a *named* discourse, analyzes that which makes our skin crawl. Phorontology is not an ism, but a *Grundrisse.* Phorontology studies that which grows from the breaks and ruptures in the ground of things. *We must begin to ask ourselves what sites we occupy. If we do not, then the current phase of hyperhistory will create a presentation or representation of "reality" that is so persuasive that we will find ourselves living under a more frightening despotic regime than ever before (I include in this statement all the current and troubling trends towards the so-called "alt-right" or neo-fascist political parties or movements that have been emerging around the world from roughly 2014 to the present).*[7] Check your watch and note the time.

---

7   Consider the rising popularity of Marine Le Pen's National Front in France, Norbert Hofer's Freedom Party in Austria, Geert Wilders's Party for Freedom in the Netherlands, Jimmie Akesson's Sweden Democrats, Andrej Babis in the Czech Republic, Beppe Grillo's Five Star Movement in Italy, and Frauke Petry's Alternative for Germany party. The popularity of these parties is rising after the Brexit vote in June of 2016 (in which Britain exited the European Union) and the unprecedented and rather surreal presidential win of Donald Trump in the United States.

The Site

T HE ROOT OF SUBJECTIVITY DISGUISES an undiagnosed parasite, but this parasite — or the sub-type of this parasite — lies at the heart of any thing that has been thrown: any object, subject, abject, reject, deject, or transject. If this parasite is initially born within language, then its material origins can be found in the technology of the printing press. The printing press is itself a technological parasite. Consider the ways in which the material boundary of page format creates new possibilities for the production and presentation of knowledge. Thanks to the printing press, it becomes possible to cite works because of "authorial" consistency.

The Gutenberg revolution allows for the writer to compose with a consideration of *œuvre* or a complete literary history printed in simultaneity with the emergence of a new industry. In 1424, the Cambridge library housed 122 books (each of which was worth a fortune). The printing press permits the dissemination of both "the book" and also public literacy — all of which is made possible by the structure of the phonetic alphabet. I am, in part, para-citing McLuhan to make this claim.[1]

With Gutenberg's invention in 1439, he puts into process the structural constraints and parasites that provide the basis for a modern consciousness. The printing press disseminates the parasite of constraint and is an invention or discovery that permits the mass production of a "subject" — a "subject" that is likewise built upon a phenomenological site. In the same manner that Copernicus revolutionizes the relation of inside and outside, the

---

1   See Marshall McLuhan, *The Gutenberg Galaxy: The Making of Typographic Man* (Toronto: University of Toronto Press, 2002).

printing press revolutionizes conceptions of psychic constraint, including cultural norms, intellectual heritage, and social lineage. The parasitic wasp Dinocampus coccinellae infects the spotted lady beetle Coleomeqilla maculata and injects its eggs into the beetle's abdomen where the wasp eggs feed on the beetle. Eventually, the miniature wasps hatch and exit through the exoskeleton and are protected by the beetle until they mature. The wasp and the beetle are combined through a parasitic notion of culture and society and a type of host-parasite communication.

The calligraphic presentation of writing aligns with the ways in which composition is interlinked with social status; for example, literacy was typically limited to the clergy. On the one hand, consider the socially determined inheritances of penmanship, decorated letters, and personalized seals; the computer, on the other hand, allows the writer to compose with greater *error*. Insofar as mistakes written by hand could be scratched out by quill, and its correction "inserted" above the scission, this error is then forever recorded onto the materiality of the page. In the computer age, the formatting of the page comes by way of a program and not by way of social or personal preference. The printing press creates a "historical standard" that permits the parasitic writing of what can be called "History."[2]

The technology of the press allows for the parasite of constraint to influence sociocultural modes of pattern recognition. In the current schema of postmortemism, hyperhistory is recorded everyday, by everybody. E-mail, blogs, online journals, and websites such as Facebook, Twitter, Snapchat, and Instagram each create an archive of personal life and individual history.[3] This historical situation morphs historiography into a project

2   My claims here build on the work of Walter Ong. See Chapters Four and Five of his work *Orality and Literacy: The Technologizing of the Word* (London: Routledge, 2002).

3   For some select sources that trace the lineage between the Gutenberg revolution and the emergence of new media, see Sven Birkerts's *The Gutenberg Elegies: The Fate of Reading in an Electronic Age* (New York: Farrar, Straus and Giroux, 2006); Peter Shillingsburg's *From Gutenberg to Google: Elec-*

that is rhizomatic, simultaneous, and constellational. These N-histories written by almost anyone with a cable connection, do not progress in the same way as traditionally recorded history, but rather, *constellate* and form a fractal narrative. The Internet is therefore the variegated space of a simulated continuum and, as such, it gives form to Shakespeare's spider web.[4]

If we combine this hyperhistorical archive with that of New Media, then the tally of hyperhistory becomes mind-boggling: news stations have uncountable hours of archived footage; television (with its own archived and re-run history); cinema (production company archives); and even the countless hours of footage never watched (the surveillance footage that is recorded everyday); each adds up to the hyperhistorical (or what could be called the *hyperhysterical*) fascination with the posthuman. We have entered into an era of the postmortem of the postmodern. Postmortemism is where we are: navel-gazing at our Bodies without Organs.

Our histories and media games function as technologized tools — as digital hammers and updated arrows. The tool, as the technological object, extends human consciousness (McLuhan), and in so doing, the site of consciousness becomes situated within a new relation of site and para-site. The hammer — which is the Nietzschean tool of philosophy — extends human consciousness during the formation of new sites and new parasites. This extension creates an emergent and fractal conflation. A fractal conflation builds other sites of experience that are both actual and virtual. Prior to the concept of "subjectivity," there must have been a site that permitted the emergence of a subject or self. What was this site? I doubt that this site was strictly neurological; instead, I claim that any subjective-site becomes truly "subjective" only when that site has been properly situated

---

tronic *Representations of Literary Texts* (Cambridge: Cambridge University Press, 2006).

4 This claim partly links to the work of Jussi Parikka in his book *Insect Media: An Archaeology of Animals and Technology* (Minneapolis: University of Minnesota Press, 2010). In *Insect Media,* Parikka argues that various forms of insect social organization mirror the complexity of new media.

for the entrance of a para-site. The same goes for objects: prior to objectivity, there must be a site that can situate the object as a thing in a place or space.

When considering the evolution of writing in Egypt, Harold Innis emphasizes the subjective and social importance of the transition from the stone medium to the medium of papyrus. He argues that, "'[b]y escaping from the heavy medium of stone' thought gained lightness."[5] The lighter medium of the papyrus leaf broadens the possibilities of mass consciousness: the movement between cuneiform and the hieroglyph implies a change from *singularity* to *continua*. The stone medium is unchanging and intensely tactile, demonstrating both a history and a personal consciousness delimited by a notion of singularity. Stone is not malleable, but rather, foundational. There is no play to the stone medium. The stone is substantive, singular, and unchanging, while lacking constellational significance. The continuum of the hieroglyph is contrasted to the singularity of cuneiform in that the hieroglyph (from *hieros* meaning "sacred" and *gluphē* meaning "carving") is no longer "set in stone," but becomes as malleable as the papyrus sign or the parasite-body. The influence of the previous medium resides inside the hieroglyph (folded like a Guinea worm) in that the notion of "carving" remains the basis of possible conceptions of "writing."

In our current age, the singularity of the printing press has been replaced by the binary language of the computer. Newer forms consume older forms. The very idea of "carving" is descissional in that a carving necessarily cuts potentialities out of reality — out of the continuum of experience. For what I call the *res*-of-chaos, writing and language *carve* reality from other patterns; in other words, language carves things out of chaos.

Media are chaotic things that parasitize other chaotic things: the printing press and the hieroglyph; cuneiform and architec-

---

5   Harold A. Innis, *Empire and Communications* (Toronto: Dundurn, 2007), 36.

ture; the ideogram and texture.[6] The medium of cinema for example has changed the way we think and the patterns that we recognize. The subject, when communicating with other subjects, thinks in close-ups, pans, edits, soundtracks, genres, and other conventions of entertainment. Entertainment has *entered* collective and personal consciousness — it cannot be contained. This "cinematic subject" is prone to *indivisualization* more than individuation: the individual has become indivisual in the era of entertainment media.

Cinematic technology, camera, audio, and special effects allow for an "active" subject who experiences an intensely tactile world. Tracing the lineage of cuneiform to the sound byte would demonstrate the influence of these "extensions of the human" when they are given economic reign over the patterns that code for the subject. This ontological development is very much about *situations*: situations that *situate* the subject and align him or her with a site while influencing that site with a para-site — a parasite that confines the subject within an imaginary body. There is no "self" in this model and no "I." Instead, there are only a variety of sites that code a so-called "subject" as being *of* certain sites and para-sites. This emphasized "of" that makes, in phorontology, a subject into a "subject-of" emerges across a realm of sites and para-sites through an imagined narrative coherency that disguises an underlying transjection. The phorontological transject is necessarily *thrown* into the world and operates ontologically and phenomenologically through a variety of *ofs* that shift and morph that particular transject across time and space (or place). As Heidegger points out for his theory of the being

---

6   See: Arndt Niebisch, *Media Parasites in the Early Avant-Garde: On the Abuse of Technology and Communication* (New York: Palgrave Macmillan, 2012). Niebisch proposes a parasitology of the avant-garde (13), particularly of Futurism and Dadaism, and claims that these movements repeatedly renegotiate the relationship of parasite and host (15). He writes that "[t]he parasite is nothing that invades language, but emerges in the process of reading" (62), which is a claim that I partly agree with. The parasite as such does not invade language because, in the context of *Language Parasites,* it is already endemic to the very structure of language.

of Being, the *Dasein* is thrown into the world (*geworfen*).[7] Despite his preference for etymological analyses, Heidegger does not locate his theory of *Geworfenheit* or thrownness in the etymology of "subject" or "object." However, when I use the term "thrown" I want to explicitly link it to the etymology of "subject" and "object." The word "subject" derives from *sub* or "under" and *iacere*, meaning "to cast, throw, or put." A subject is, in its very being, subservient — akin to a vassal for a feudal lord. The word "object" derives from *ob* or "towards or against" and *iacere* again. An object is a thing that is thrown before an observing mind. The very concept of an object requires an observer or an other that can legitimate its status as "object." Perhaps this is the reason why Heidegger will privilege the notion of a thing (or *das Ding*) in his later work because a thing is more "in itself" than an object. However, the concepts of the subject and the object are, according to their etymologies, necessarily thrown into being and language. Therefore, I privilege thrownness in a non-Heideggerian or post-Heideggerian fashion: thrownness is the essential state of an object or a subject and thrownness designates the basic status of being an entity. A transject is, like a subject and an object, thrown into being, but it is a being that is thrown into a space that resides in between subject and object — the transject resists and rejects the requirements of power that position and site the subject as disempowered and also the observing mind that brings the object into existence. As a combinant entity, the transject exists as that which transfers and transitions between subjects and objects, abjects and projects, dejects and rejects. The transject is the localized entity of a drastically anterior — anterior to the "human" — notion of Being. The transject is the local face of the xenoject. The emergence of the transject will be explained in further detail throughout this book, but currently, in this chapter, only the surface level of its language will be considered.

---

7   Martin Heidegger, *Being and Time,* trans. John Macquarrie and Edward Robinson (New York: HarperPerennial, 2008), 223. I highlight one page here, but Heidegger uses the concept throughout *Being and Time.*

What Herder calls **Homo loquens** describes the human ability to *interact with and produce a world of signs.* Semiotics is the study of signs and signs themselves are always written or scored into media. Cuneiform, glyph, paper, or cyberspace are each media-sites occupied by signs. A sign requires a site to become situated. If there were no site that could situate a sign, then that sign would cease to exist. The site in turn sites itself as the site of a sign. A site is known if it can be sited by signs that live parasitically *inside it.* A site is always, by definition, somewhat parasitic. In this context, a site is only partly pre-linguistic and also post-linguistic in that nothing can be "known" or communicated without a siting-language. The signs of language deposit meaning in and onto a site, but this "depositing" does not occur without an informational positing — a positing that results in the positioning of language and then the siting of the sited in the site.

Phorontology studies the sites and para-sites that are created and produced by the complex interplay of transjects, subjects, objects, worlds, and signs. These sites of complexity are built in response to a variety of different collisions between levels and disciplines: there are, for example, political sites, sacred sites, cultural sites, social sites, or many others. Each site is ontologically "clarified" in relation to its grounding or foundational para-site.

Where can the site or para-site be located in the parasitic dynamic produced in Raymond Queneau's 1961 work *Cent mille milliards de poèmes*? Queneau creates his poetry experiment out of ten original sonnets in which all of the fourteen lines from each sonnet could be re-assembled to create 100,000,000,000,000 new sonnets (because $10^{14} = 100,000,000,000,000$). This permutational text is, in a sense, the longest book every written — even if its length is primarily virtual. It would be impossible to read every possible iteration of Queneau's text in a human lifetime because it would take some 200,000,000 years to read every possible poem — even while reading for twenty-four hours a day. Queneau's project depicts a kind of virtual parasitism in which the parasite of constraint creates a multiplicity of repetition. The para-sites extend from the site and write themselves into potential spaces and readers.

Space is not place. Geography writes a place onto a space. When a space becomes a place it is written upon and signed by a kind of "author": a "place" is created through the complex interplay of constraint and site. Why? Sites are generative locales in that they generate other sites. A place exists, in phorontology, in *potentia* because a site is required before a space can become a spacing and before something — literally a *some-thing* — can be placed inside a space. Without a site, or without the signs that can sign, assign, or design a site, a place cannot emerge from a space. In this context, a space is vacuous — a vacuum — an emptiness.

Food

Eating food is the moment of a direct encounter with an Other — with a Lacanian real or with a violating abject. For this reason, phorontology does not only study sites, but also the *consumption* that occurs in sites. Of course commodities are consumed and various other objects of exchange, but these objects or things — when consumed — produce both information and energy: objects or things of consumption fill the body and mind of the host-subject with forces that are simultaneously symbiotic and parasitic. In the present day, food is a rem(a)inder of an abject experience of bodily functions because food triggers an overstimulated awareness of bodily organs and anatomy — an anatomy of intensity.

There is no barrier or boundary, in phorontology, between the subject, the object, the other, or the Body without Organs: each of these concepts represent a fractal-continuum of embodiment through which and upon which various discourses are forcibly inscribed. Food is all that is left, not the consumer. The term "*sitos*" does not necessarily signify "food," but rather the *sign of the site*. Sites are signs at the same time that they are signed. Certain sites are signed as "subjects." The so-called "subject" has progressed through a variety of historical and epis-

temic formations: *Cogito,* transcendental, existential, phenomenological, psychoanalytic, semiotic, nihilist, and many others.
The totality of this continuum captures what I mean by "site."
For this reason, we need a phorontology: an analytical approach
that is attuned to the parasitic and the non-human. Phorontology emphasizes *input* or *intake* more than "output."

Sex

Andrea Dworkin relates sex with violation in *Intercourse* (1987):
for Dworkin, every sex act is an act of violation or rape for the
woman. Human sexuality becomes, for Dworkin, the equivalent
of bed bug sex — a violent encounter where the penis is wielded
as a knife and stabbed into the womb. An alternative theory of
parasite-sex can be found in the writings of Shannon Bell. In
Bell's *Fast Feminism* (2010), the sexual act becomes an experience of pure complementarity where both partners occupy the
position of what gets called the "phallus" in psychoanalysis. Bell
suggests that a vagina is an inverted phallus (usually much larger than an actual penis), so that during intercourse the man's
phallus fucks the woman's inner phallus that is similarly fucking
the man's, thereby creating a folded sexuality of situational complementarity. No one is ever fully "on top" because both parties engage in a spiraling parasite-discourse where passion and
pleasure fold in a fractal of unmitigated squirt and ejaculate. Sex
is liquid and cannot be sited. Parasites are folds.

"Madness"

Even a cursory glance through the DSM-IV and V demonstrates
that so-called "mental illnesses" are *spectrum disorders* that become privy to positions or sitings upon a continuum of mental
states. The DSM-IV and V reinstate ontological thought within a
"zero degree" of consciousness that resides somewhere outside
of its pages, not within its bindings or on the street. The DSM-
IV and V present not only a continuum of "mental illness," but
also a continuum of consciousness *as site*. The site of conscious-

ness — which I call "the metafractal" — is inscribed with various subject-ofs that momentarily "fix" or construct that site as discursive. This discursivity is, through repetition, normalized when it becomes a morphogenetic or logogenetic "building" or "structure." Both the body and mind become engaged in a type of molecular and molar continuum where delineations between micro and macro processes are rendered fractal.

Miscellany

Phorontology studies the language site(s) and the emergent para-site(s) of language: it is a theory that we presume to "eat," but it simultaneously eats us. Phorontology is an attempt to begin to analyze these intrusions or "sitings" that we call "subject" and "object" — sitings that provide "grounds" for given structures, such as the psychic, the familial, the sexual, the textual, the political, the cultural, the historical, etc. Every intrusion is a sited and situated rem(a)inder of fragility amidst the visible and paravisible structures that define our words and worlds.

The Para-site

Phorontology studies its own parasite: *the Parasite of Language.* This parasite has gradually infected human consciousness and evolved throughout human history. What I call the "para-site" permits the potential of *para-sight,* which denotes the virtual and yet visual regimes that reside *beside* traditional practices of seeing. The term "parasite of constraint" is exceptional and ex-centric in that any para-site is, by definition, an *exception* to a given site.

Finding the Parasite

Writing is fundamentally parasitic. Jacques Derrida argues that "the literally Saussurian formulas reappear within the question of the relationships between speech and writing: the order of writing is the order of exteriority, of the 'occasional,' of the 'accessory,' of the 'auxiliary,' of the '*parasitic*.'"[1] Writing feeds on previous writing(s) and consumes earlier writing through a progressive literary history. The "parasite of language" is *inside* language and feeds beside other writing within a symbiotic relationship. In this sense, every "new" text is new only in its proximity to an earlier writing — in its essentially parasitic nature or in the efficiency of its *para-*status. In other words, a writing becomes "literary" by virtue of the effectiveness of its "living beside."

---

1   Jacques Derrida, *Of Grammatology: Corrected Edition,* trans. Gayatri Chakravorty Spivak (Baltimore: Johns Hopkins University Press, 1997), 54.

"Writing" and "subjectivity" are two concepts that are constituted by self-reflexive or self-referential structures. The reflexivity that is necessary for the production of a "writing" or "self" is either the result of an evolutionary accident, an underlying glitch of "wiring," or an undiagnosed parasitic illness. Lacan likes insisting that "it speaks,"[2] by which he means that language speaks. The only way that the "unconscious could be structured *like* a language"[3] (in Lacan's timeless refrain), is if language is, at its basis, parasitic; put differently, somewhere *inside* language (if language indeed has an "inside"), there resides a folded parasite that frequently masquerades as the "Other." This "Other" no doubt provides a sense of coherency to subjectivity by virtue of its *feeding schedule* in which the "Other" — as a symptom — consumes a little of the ontological nutrition that has been ear-marked for the stability of the subject. The "Other" does not only provide a sense of "completion" for the subject because the "Other" — which in Lacan is sometimes synonymous with "language" or with the symbolic order — has essentially *re-wired* the subject to require the Other-as-parasite. The Other *lives beside* the subject as a kind of language and this Other functions parasitically at a location that is found at a *para-site* to the human. This model describes a metaphysical instance of the host-parasite (or host and guest) relationship.

Derrida already proposes a kind of linguistic parasite — a particularly Derridean genus of the language parasite. The genus that I am proposing is different from Derrida's (and also Serres's — but I will explore Serres more fully in the final chapter). Derrida writes that "if one knew perfectly well what one thought and stated while assuring that one learns to write *after* having learned to speak, would that suffice to conclude that what thus comes 'after' is parasitic? And what is a parasite? And

---

2   Jacques Lacan, *Écrits: The First Complete Edition in English,* trans. Bruce Fink in collaboration with Héloïse Fink and Russell Grigg (New York: Norton, 2006), 578.

3   Jacques Lacan, *The Seminar of Jacques Lacan: On Feminine Sexuality, The Limits of Love and Knowledge: Book xx: Encore 1972–1973,* ed. Jacques-Alain Miller, trans. Bruce Fink (New York: Norton, 1999), 48. Original emphasis.

if writing were precisely that which makes us reconsider our logic of the parasite?"[4] If the parasite of language appears "after" the subject has learned to speak, then that would suggest that the parasite *infects* the subject after the subject's emergence into the symbolic order — into language. I do not see why Derrida would privilege speech over writing in terms of his definition of the parasitic (unless he is applying Saussure's logic to a thinking about the parasitic), but perhaps any engagement with language qua language would render the subject as a host; in other words, the subject would become a host once language has somehow entered the body (or mind).

However, this model need not be teleological; there need not be a definitive beginning — particularly, if human beings are **Homo loquens**. Writing would then offer a variety of representations, simulations, or maskings for the parasite. Temporally speaking, a language parasite would exist *beyond* time. As Lacan and Freud suggest, there is no time in the unconscious and if the unconscious is structured like a language (or, more precisely like a language that is constructed on the basis of a parasitic infection — a kind of metaphysical infection), then the parasite itself would be, in a sense, infinite, immortal, or timeless. Because of the odd and surprising qualities of this metaphysical parasite a variety of alternative therapies are required: a dash of 'Pataphysics, a smattering of non-philosophy, and a sprinkle of philosophical speculation. The infection exists in the words that I use to describe myself. The infection lives inside the words that I use on this page. The infection resides inside the stories and linguistic memories that compose a "self." We cannot escape this parasite. The comedian Steven Wright once said: "I wish my first word as a baby was 'quote' so that my last word could be 'unquote.'" Everything in between the quote and the unquote is partly permitted by the parasite that allows the host's speech — a parasite that permits a self that claims selfhood. This parasite speaks through *me*, writes with *my fingers* that move on this letter pad, and it partly claims my name. My name, for example, is

---

4   Derrida, *Of Grammatology,* 54.

simply one textual iteration that "claims" authority over a text in a long line of textual iterations — iterations that have been permitted by the referentiality intrinsic to the linguistic parasites.

In *Limited Inc* from 1988, Derrida's essay "Signature Event Context" (originally from 1972) has a subsection entitled: "Parasites. Iter, of Writing: That It Perhaps Does Not Exist." In this essay, Derrida is responding to J.L. Austin's *How to Do Things with Words* (1975) based on Austin's lectures at Harvard University in 1955. Derrida points out that Austin situates some aspects of language as being constituted by an exclusion — an exclusion that remains "*abnormal*" and "*parasitic*" (original emphasis).[5] Perhaps this abnormal and parasitic exclusion is partly "performative." According to Derrida, the performative utterance "does not describe something that exists outside of language and prior to it."[6] Indeed, this exterior and anticipatory language would be closer to (but not the same as) what Derrida calls "arche-writing." From a phorontological approach, what Derrida calls "arche-writing" describes a writing that simultaneously occupies a site and also *multiple other sites*. What could be called the "ontology" of this language parasite — the term "parasite" is being used here in its ontogenetic, singular usage — would occupy a site that is *para* to another site.

The site itself (when it is not a para-site) can be considered as being open to signification, but this claim is only true if the signs that fill a site remain provisional so that a site can be named repeatedly. Sites and para-sites emerge from spaces and places and function according to a version of Freud's theory of *Wiederholungzwang* in which the site would occasionally return as a place or a space (while not being confined to the ontological descriptors or boundaries of either "place" or "space"). The site can sometimes be language-based, but the language that fills a site also allows for the emergence of a subject — a subject that is embodied, affective, written, spoken, and lived. Language is

---

5   Jacques Derrida, *Limited Inc,* trans. Jeffrey Mehlman (Evanston: Northwestern University Press, 1988), 16.

6   Ibid., 13.

lived *through* as media and, as media, language acts as the interface between a subject-as-host (a subject-of or a transject) and the parasite (of constraint, of language, or of a para-site). McLuhan famously argues that "the medium is the message," but now his claim can be parasitized as what it always was: *the HOST-medium is the PARASITE-message.*

However, if the medium has become a host (or if it always was a host) to a parasite-message (a message that may have always been parasitic), then what can be done to cure the sick contemporary subject of her or his infection? Derrida cites a moment from J.L. Austin where Austin suggests that language consists of a flowering quality: language "is in special ways […], parasitic upon its normal use — ways which fall under the doctrine of the *etiolations* of language."[7] A plant is said to be "etiolated" when it grows in a space that either has partial or no light. The related meaning of "etiolate" as pallid or feeble builds on this initial definition because etiolated plants grow in spindly ways — in order to reach any available light — and result in a pale color. Considering language as a flowering entity or words as flowers has a long history that I will selectively para-cite here: the tenth century poet Ki no Yoshimochi (who died c. 919) used the character for flower (*hana* 華) to mean poetic words.[8] Many poets and thinkers consider a poetic word to be both a word and a flower: for example, the German Romantic poet Friedrich Hölderlin, like Ki no Yoshimochi, argues that language is "die Blume des Mundes" (or "the flower of the mouth") and he also writes, "Worte, wie Blumen" (or "words, like flowers").[9] In this sense, Austin is using the word "etiolation" to suggest an im-

7   Quoted in ibid., 16. See J.L. Austin, *How to Do Things with Words* (Cambridge: Harvard University Press, 1975), 21–22, for the original reference.
8   See Michael F. Marra, "Things and Words," in *Japan's Frames of Meaning: A Hermeneutics Reader,* ed. Michael F. Marra, 3–50 (Honolulu: University of Hawai'i Press, 2011), 36.
9   Quoted in Paul Ricoeur, *The Rule of Metaphor: The Creation of Meaning in Language,* trans. Robert Czerny with Kathleen McLaughlin and John Costello, SJ (London: Routledge, 2003), 335. Ricoeur is para-citing Hölderlin as quoted in Martin Heidegger, *Unterwegs zur Sprache* (Frankfurt am Main: Vittorio Klostermann, 1985), 194 and 195 resp. A chain of para-cites.

proper growth in the flowering of language — a kind of illness that he sees as being "parasitic."

I would push this dynamic further and say that the *etiolations of language require an etiology.* Does language flower? If it flowers, then it flowers in a virtual space — as either a rhizome or an arborescence. This virtual space functionally *sites* language and it is from this other space that language enters the subject. Phorontology offers a first attempt at a differential diagnosis on the illness that lurks within language.

Part of the problem with properly locating and diagnosing the language parasite (or the language parasites) is that language is occasionally performative. Not only is the language that the subject uses oftentimes performative, but the subject is herself or himself performative in that both language and subjectivity perform a model (or modality) of *health*. It is only at limit experiences of both language and subjectivity that the symptomatology of the parasitic illness begins to reveal itself. This parasite-host model of language and the "self" transforms ontology into a very strange discipline because the limitations or borders of "Being" become fuzzy and indeterminate. Heidegger's use of the term *Sein* (as "being") is materially rendered on the page as a sign. *Sein* is a sign. Unfortunately, the writing of "Being" as a sign devalues or discredits the possibility of an authentic relationship to *Sein* because the writing of *Sein* as a sign distances the host from her or his "self" and resituates the host-parasite relationship as one that privileges the parasite. The parasite that lives inside language exists as a medium: it is a medium through which subjects say or write "I." The medium of the parasite is cursory, elusive, and, like Being, (en)folded.

Derrida writes that Austin prefers to exclude "the general theory of this structural parasitism"[10] in favor of a meditation on the anomalies, infelicities, and exceptions of writing. Regardless, a general theory of "structural parasitism" is very much at issue in deconstruction and I would prefer not to reject or repress the potentialities offered by parasitic structure. However,

---

10   Derrida, *Limited Inc,* 16.

what if the issue is not structural parasitism as such, but rather what lives *inside* structure? Structure is not a parasite because the parasite is what permits a thinking and a writing of structure. If this claim is correct, then structure contains the parasitic within it — it already contains the poststructural, but a feedback loop is present even here because the poststructural — when it is parasitic, is, precisely speaking, proto-structural. The deconstructive parasite is certainly poststructural, but this entity is not the only philosophical parasite that lurks in the regimes of human and posthuman thought: there is also a proto-structural parasite — a parasite that permits the emergence of structure.

To that end, phorontology does not pursue a structural parasitism because structure conceals its own lack of a parasite. Instead, phorontology interrogates the existence of a proto-structural parasite — a parasite that lays hidden inside language, inside being, and inside thought. An etiology is certainly required to approach this proto-structural parasite. The appropriate etiology is likely parallactic; an etiology that is able to consider proto-structural parasitism from a perspective that is "awry" to traditional modes of seeing and analysis. In other words, a para-sight is required to diagnose a para-site. This heretical approach can partly be found in 'Pataphysics, but not even in traditional 'Pataphysics.

Feeding the Parasite

Christopher Dewdney ends his poetry book, *Alter Sublime* (1980), with a 'pataphysical study entitled "Parasite Maintenance." Dewdney offers a speculative writing of exceptions that can better diagnose the genus of the language-parasite and the parasite of constraint. 'Pataphysics is Alfred Jarry's term for a "science of imaginary solutions" — a science that exists beyond physics and metaphysics as an absurdist science of the combinant discourse that arises from the collision of the *meta* and the *para.*[11] When *meta* and *para* combine, they produce the *pata*. Jarry's 'Pataphysics is a science of exceptions and a science of epiphenomena — it approaches topics not through a consideration of their phenomena (as in phenomenology for example), but rather, through their unconsidered and mysterious entryways and exits. 'Pataphysics is a discourse of exceptional epiphenomenology and Dewdney concludes his poetry book with an epiphenomenological engagement with the language parasite.

Dewdney does not offer a general theory of structural parasitism (which is what Derrida is against) because he prefers a general theory of proto-structural parasitism: he begins to reveal the language parasite through its own available contours and weaknesses:

[T]he evolution of language, inextricably bound with the evolution of our consciousness as a species, has diverged from its parallel & dependent status with the human species and has become "animated," i.e. has, much like a model of artificial intelligence, or a robot, taken on a life of its own. Furthermore, I propose that special linguistic qualities peculiar to the English language, indicate the existence of a "Governor" (in a mechanistic sense) with which the "animated" language acts on the individual, restricting the limits of conceptualization.[12]

Dewdney situates the language-parasite in historical terms in much the same way as William Burroughs does in *The Ticket That Exploded* (1962/1967). In *Ticket,* Burroughs asserts that either "language is a virus" or "the word is now a virus,"[13] a thought that anticipates Dewdney's conception of language as an exterior parasitical force that effectively infects its host. Dewdney's

11 Alfred Jarry, *Exploits & Opinions of Dr. Faustroll, Pataphysician,* trans. Simon Watson Taylor (Boston: Exact Change, 1996), 21–24.
12 Christopher Dewdney, "Parasite Maintenance," in *Alter Sublime,* 75–92 (Toronto: Coach House, 1980), 75.
13 William S. Burroughs, *The Ticket That Exploded* (New York: Grove, 1992), 49.

appraisal of "the Governor,"[14] by which he means an operative, controlling force — a notion comparable to Burroughs's "operator" — is controlled by a Parasite. The structure of this model is akin to Burroughs's understanding of writing as a parasitic procedure — a practice also found in the postmodern stylings that exude from the posthumanistic stench that wafts around after the death of the Lyotardian *grand récits*.

In the posthuman or the postmodern, there may be a "Governor" who re-instates systems of legitimation — systems of "normalcy." The posthuman subject or historically determinate transject perceives external phenomena as stimuli and filters these stimuli into a simulacrum of appearances that is hegemonically coded as "reality." I call this process of reality production or reality normalization *indivisualization.* The transject becomes normalized as a "subject-of" when indivisualization takes hold; however, this indivisualizing process is not "individual" per se, but prone to the whims and preferences of the underlying language-parasite.

Minds are notoriously adaptive: patients who have lesions in the Broca region of the brain experience neuroplastic re-wiring as neurons determine new pathways around lesions. The brain develops newer and different wrinkles. In the case of a reality simulation, these neural delineations are necessarily ideological and mythocryptic, effectively forging perception through the codes and messages of the language-parasite. Such "ideological delineations" are the result of the dictates of what Dewdney calls the "Governor":

Finally I also posit that the specialized use of linguistic inventions by the poet enables him to transcend the domain of the "Governor," through the use of a *special neural system* singular to the ontogeny of the writer. This structure or system, a special condition of intelligence outside the realm of

---

14 In an uncanny echo, Serres also says: "Let us return to the paralytic, that is to say, to the governor." See Michel Serres, *The Parasite,* trans. Lawrence R. Schehr (Minneapolis: University of Minnesota Press, 2007), 36.

both the "animated" language & the "Governor," I refer to as the Parasite.[15]

Dewdney's formulation articulates in depth a 'pataphysical appraisal of what the "subject" has become in the contemporary era. The "subject" is never centralized or stabilized because it is always "of" various forces — an exterior Governor or an anterior Parasite.

When Marx famously describes ideology as functioning on the basis of the aphorism: "Sie wissen das nicht, aber sie tun es," which is translated by Žižek as "they do not know it, but they are doing it,"[16] Dewdney will later 'pataphysically hone in on the specific ways in which ideology is something that "they do not know that they do." For Dewdney, "language presupposes a special barrier, generally beyond perception, which precludes certain higher forms of conceptual reasoning from the age of verbal consciousness forward. This barrier is *the Governor,* and the success of the antenna to a large degree depends on the complex battle between *the Parasite* and *the Governor.*"[17] Dewdney's binaristic schema of "Parasite" and "Governor" mirrors a kind of host and parasite or host and guest dynamic in which power is shared between both parties like Hegel's dialectical analysis of the master and the slave. Like the master and the slave, the Governor and the Parasite function in an undecidable power differential without terminus — there is no decision in the dynamic of host and parasite. The host and the parasite share positions in which both parasite each other — they parasite each other through the multidirectional quality of power. However, the dyad of Governor and Parasite also inaugurates another binary: that of inside and outside. The Governor is the host of the inside to the parasite's exteriority. Even this moment denies closure or a decision though because the parasite is complex and utterly liminal — truly transject. The parasite enters the host from the

---

15 Dewdney, "Parasite," 75–76. Emphasis added.
16 Slavoj Žižek, *The Sublime Object of Ideology* (London: Verso, 1989), 28.
17 Dewdney, "Parasite," 78.

outside, but it then functions as an inside, or as an outside that has become an inside. Therefore, the Governor or host is typically an inside while the Parasite is transjected — a folded entity that is both outside and inside. It transitions and shifts and cannot be located or sited at either an inside or an outside: it is, for this reason, a Parasite that lives at a para-site. The outside that becomes an inside only to transition again to another outside — that model is the parasite as proto-structure. The parasite itself offers a proto-structure as a kind of morphogenetic field from which hosts and Governors emerge. The Parasite, for Dewdney, permits original and novel forms of autopoiesis (the term for organic self-organization): "I will speak of *the Parasite* as an internal structure generating novel configurations. It is the *origin* of these signals that is outside."[18]

The Parasite terminologically locates the origin of a fold or the combination or 'pataphysical collision of exterior and interior. The Dewdneyan Parasite is an aporia *par excellence*. I remember reading that Burroughs once asked: "which came first the tapeworm or the intestine?" A parasite body (such as a tapeworm that lines the small intestine) enfolds itself so effectively that the notion of an inside or an outside — an inside of the host or parasite or the outside of the host or parasite — becomes undecidable. The Parasite negates the firmament of any decision.[19] The Laruellean decision is resisted and the Parasite becomes a Derridean undecidable. This process gives birth to a variety of surprising and strange entities — a panoply of transjected beings. The emergence of this bizarre army of beings that push beyond formerly fixed definitions of Being require a careful phorontological analysis.

---

18 Dewdney, "Parasite," 78.
19 I mean "decision" in Laruellean terms. John Mullarkey and Anthony Paul Smith point out that, for Laruelle, "[d]ecision, then, is the invariant structure of philosophy. To 'decide' is to cut oneself off from the Real, to represent it." See John Mullarkey and Anthony Paul Smith, "Introduction: The Non-Philosophical Inversion: Laruelle's Knowledge Without Domination," in *Laruelle and Non-Philosophy,* eds. John Mullarkey and Anthony Paul Smith, 1–18 (Edinburgh: Edinburgh University Press, 2012), 7.

Dewdney offers a provisional assessment of the anatomy of the language parasite and he models it after geology. For Dewdney, the language parasite has the soft body parts of a decaying fish where "it is as if the fish's flesh was continuously re-assembled, fossilized particle by particle, morpheme-connotation by morpheme-connotation, over centuries of change in the living language; a living fossil whose flesh transubstantiates itself in the wind of dialectic modification."[20] The parts of the language parasite accumulate to compose the totality of the etiolated language. This Dewdneyan geological consideration of language's etiolations activates related theories of sediment. The notion of a fossilized history is very important for North American poetics: Steve McCaffery's *Theory of Sediment* (1992) and Dewdney's own *The Natural History* (2002) and *A Palaeozoic Geology of London, Ontario* (1974) each deal with the fossilization of history.

The concept of "sediment" — of a properly linguistic sediment — registers, for Dewdney, language as a "House" of "living language." In this framework, language is conceived of as a construction — a construction that is built upon a site. Language is built upon a site, but it also accrues its own geological — or 'pataphysically geological — version of sediment. In her work *Meddle English* (2011), the poet Caroline Bergvall, like Dewdney, conceives of language in geological or sedimentary terms. In *Meddle English,* Bergvall begins to excavate the various layers of language-as-geology: "Principally, one discovers surprising varietals of soil, ancient yet compilable language bones, pressed word-fossils, collapsed layers, mineral toil, friable clays, dried pigments, decomposed fabric stretches, discontinuous tracings, and much unrecoverable matter."[21] Bergvall 'pataphysically specifies that, in this geological "house," "[t]he top layers reveal a far larger extent of familiar elements, traceable glossary, well-defined graphemes, syllabic conduits, what looks like mud-encased capitalizations, gold-dust, systems of numerical sticks,

---

20 Dewdney, "Parasite," 81.
21 Caroline Bergvall, *Meddle English: New and Selected Texts* (Callicoon: Nightboat Books, 2011), 6.

animal feathers, and various types of tools. These trace up letter elements historically, and through the altogether confusing and inventive arche-logics of etymology. Language is its own midden ground."[22] Both Dewdney's "house" and Bergvall's "midden ground" deploy building and geological metaphors to describe language — they describe language's "body" with metaphors that are composed of language. The parasite curls in on itself. The noise of language — its feedback-like recursivity — trails the tapeworm's tail back into its scolex-mouth like an Ouroboros.

However, Dewdney is not only being metaphorical because his notion of language's "house" is partly material: "The modified interpretive cortex and speech centre together make up the House of the living language."[23] I consider Dewdney's phrase the "House of the living language" an homage to Heidegger who, in his "Letter on Humanism," writes that "Being is the *House* of language."[24] Both "houses" are "built" upon the site of a *living history* — a history that is constructed and fossilized as language. Fossils pile onto each other and eventually become sediment.

For Dewdney, the "House of the living language" is the site that becomes the Parasite: "In a brain junta whose generals are the neurotransmitters, the House of the living language takes the final step and becomes the Parasite."[25] Dewdney's 'pataphysical speculations trace the ontological entifications of language: he analyzes the variegations of language's transitional sites. In other words, language is sometimes a "House of living language," or sometimes a geological quarry; at other times, language is a Governor, and at still other times, language is a Parasite. What makes Dewdney's speculation notable is that he traces the evolution of language from the Governor to the Parasite. This evolution is made possible by virtue of neuroplasticity: "The manner in which the House of the living language evolves

---

22 Ibid., 6.
23 Dewdney, "Parasite," 85.
24 Martin Heidegger, "Letter on Humanism," *Basic Writings,* trans. Frank A. Capuzzi in collaboration with J. Glenn Gray, 213–66 (New York: HarperCollins, 1993), 217.
25 Dewdney, "Parasite," 85.

into the Parasite hinges on neurotransmitters & axonal / dendritic growth,"[26] Dewdney writes.

The "House of the living language" is in some ways a reference to the neuroplastic structures of the brain and in other ways the phrase is an abstraction, but it is an abstraction that denotes a paradoxically present materiality — the materiality of language itself. Language becomes "matter" when the Parasite is unearthed from the fossilized depths of language. The Parasite is partly a name for the repressed awareness of language's inherent materiality, while the Governor maintains a definition of the sign as immaterial. Dewdney offers a 'pataphysical assessment of the ways in which the Parasite emerges from neurochemistry:

> [I]t seems reasonable to assume that the neurotransmitters whose altered levels determine the boundary of the Parasite would also be memory specific, ie; with axonal tracts & pathways connected to the hippocampus, a structure integral to both the storing and retrieval of memory in the brain. [...] These neurotransmitters are Norepinephrine and Acetycholine. I include Seratonin with these also, not because it is memory specific, but because of its association with consciousness and mind. The altered levels of norepinephrine, acetycholine and seratonin in the formative Parasite, mediated by elevated levels of camp, give rise to cascade reactions which in turn re-figure the House of the living language.[27]

These "cascade reactions" in turn transform the "House of the living language" into the Governor and then later into the Parasite. However, even though these concepts transition into each other, they each remain operative in each other at the same time. In other words, each concept depicts a different modality of the underlying parasite. The Governor is one "face" of the parasite, the "House of the living language" is one "face" of the parasite," and the Parasite is also another "face." In *The Immacu-*

---

26 Ibid., 86.
27 Ibid., 90.

late Perception (1985), Dewdney explicitly asserts that language is a self-replicating organism:

> Once conceived, language became self-replicating, a lexical organism imbedded in the species. The evolution of language, inextricably bound with the evolution of our consciousness as a species, has diverged from its parallel status and taken on a life of its own. Language is virtually an independent intelligence utilizing humans as neural components in a vast and inconceivable sentience. The living language exists symbiotically with the human "host."[28]

The parasitic nature of language is concealed by its various guises: the "House of the living language" contains a different emphasis than the Parasite or the Governor. The "House of the living language" houses both Being and beings and within this linguistic spectrum various other entities begin to appear. The Governor is the superegoic manifestation of the parasite — it connotes the ideological and hegemonic qualities of sociocultural dominance as solidified through language. The Parasite itself is the announced goal of this 'pataphysical speculation — of this phorontology. Each concept is a different coloring of the linguistically parasitic.

In Dewdney's model, folding and folded tapeworms of *langue* wrap around your cerebral cortex and they replicate themselves through self-reflexive actions and reactions — they react to the slightest hint that the subject may claim its own sovereignty. In interview with Lola Lemire Tostevin, Dewdney clarifies what he means by the terms "Governor" and "Parasite":

> What I mean by that is that anybody who uses words, and words are perverse, anybody composing art using words eventually begins to develop a perceptual appendix or addendum. Because language is so close to consciousness, this

---

eventually becomes a parasitic relationship where language spills over the bounds of reference and takes on a quasi-magical existence in consciousness as if it had more capability than it actually does. You sort of have a working neurosis at that point and that's what I mean by parasite. What the writer does with that particular language parasite, and which we all have to a certain extent, is that the dynamics of the relationship keeps the writer occupied which is like wax in the ears so that you can't hear the sirens[.][29]

Agency resides with the Parasite more than with the subject that has become a subject-of. Language and subjectivity combine and have become interlinked, thereby transferring agency between each dyadic figure: agency transfers from the subject to language and from language to the subject. When Tostevin asks Dewdney how the Parasite is "the function of language?," Dewdney responds that "[i]t's an affliction, a language affliction. But of course in the essay I go on to say that language thinks us too. Which is a pretty obvious, straight forward point to make I suppose."[30] *Language thinks*. If a parasite "lives" inside the "living language," then language begins to think the subject, to dream the subject. The subject becomes a host for language when the subject becomes *subject-of*— subject-of language or subject-of a word-parasite.

The mimetic qualities of language ontologically reinforce specific communicational behavior patterns and these patterns become normalized over time. Even though this claim may more easily and obviously align with a Lacanian framework in which agency resides with language because language is the "house" of the unconscious, I would point to a more uncanny and surprising association — that of Chomskyan linguistics. Chomsky argues in *Language and Mind* (1968) that every human being has a genetic, unconsciously hardwired ability to under-

---

29 Christopher Dewdney, "Interview with Christopher Dewdney," *Open Letter,* 7, no. 7 (1990): 84–95, at 86.

30 Ibid., 86–87.

stand language.[31] If language is "universal," then its universality must rely on its capabilities to remain hidden beyond binaristic thought. Language would then occupy a middle ground space (or continuum of spaces, places, sites, and para-sites) that exists in between subjects and objects or selves and others. Derrida quite rightly focuses on the aporic in language and on the proto-structural character of *différance* because these concepts each point to the universality of the language-parasite — to the universality of its shielded or bizarre materiality. If I may heretically collide Chomsky with Lacan for a moment, then I would argue that Chomsky's notion of "universal grammar" would require a "section of the cortex" that functions in conjunction with the accumulation of mimetic signals that could more effectively construct the socially permissible (and hegemonic) codifications of the symbolic order, which would also manifest as the exteriorized being of the parasite. In both Chomskyan and Lacanian models, language can be interpreted as the production of an underlying, invasive "parasite." Even though this claim may seem utterly against Chomsky's own theoretical allegiances, he himself claims in a lecture at Google that

> what you predict is that some other principle *external* to language, maybe some principle of nature, principle of computational efficiency or something like that which is not specific to language, interacted with a small mutation which just gave rise to the universal grammar. [...] Once the small mutation took place given this operation, recursive enumeration operation, that allows you to create a discrete infinity, [...] changing something in someone's genome and spreading through the small breeding group.[32]

---

31 Noam Chomsky, *Language and Mind* (Cambridge: Cambridge University Press, 2006), 77, 100, 106–13.
32 Noam Chomsky, "Authors@Google: Noam Chomsky," April 25, 2008, http://www.youtube.com/watch?v=rnLWSC5p1XE. The quotation begins at 12:40 in the timestamp of the video and continues to 15:44. Emphasis added.

Therefore, even Chomsky, when provided with the speculative venue of an improvised lecture, is willing to consider the possibility that language is the result of an intrinsic mutation. In Dewdneyan terms, the mutation itself may be the result of the language-parasite. If these speculations are correct, then language is the result of a parasitic rewiring and, if the Governor and the Parasite are as intertwined as Dewdney suggests, then it is likely that sentience is also the result of this mutation (Chomsky), virus (Burroughs), or parasite (Dewdney).

The very idea of a parasite conveys an ontology and an embodiment that is paradoxical, liminal, and aporic. The concept of the parasite bridges the boundaries between self and other because for the parasite there is no inside or outside: a parasite is both in the host, in the self, and in the other; as well, the parasite contains a kind of self that interlinks with the host's self. The end effect of binaristic thought processes is the concretization of the Governor and not the diagnosis of the Parasite. What we need now is a transjected re-theorization or "rewiring" of subjectivity that can begin to approach language as a parasite so that the parasite that simultaneously lurks inside (and as) consciousness will also be revealed.

Tempting the Parasite

Christian Bök theorizes a different type of 'pataphysical parasitism combined with poetics in his essay "The Xenotext Experiment" (2008) and its related project.[33] Bök intends to embed a poem inside a bacterium — inside the bacterium's genome sequences — in such a way that the bacterium will "write" a poem in response to the embedded poem that, when decoded through the alphabetic-gene cipher, will also be sensible. Bök has chosen to embed the poem in the hardy extremophile bacterium **Deinococcus radiodurans** so that the poem can live

---

33 Bök intends to release the project in two volumes. The first volume — which acts as a grimoire or trailer for the second volume — was released in 2015. See Christian Bök, *The Xenotext: Book 1* (Toronto: Coach House, 2015).

forever — as an immortal poem — beyond the death of our solar system's sun or in the empty vacuum of space. **Deinococcus radiodurans** does not die in these environments, but can survive and even thrive in the harshest of living conditions: the stubbornness of this bacterium makes it the ideal vessel for what could be, if successful, an eternal poem.

Bök claims that the poem he embeds will be the "masculine" counterpart to the bacterium's "feminine" response,[34] but I prefer to think of the differential of this relationship in different terms: the message passed between the poem and the bacterium is less an anthropocentric dynamic of sociocultural gendering and more akin to the muttering of host to parasite and parasite to host. The gendering of each poetic sequence is less fitting than a consideration of the dynamic as a parasitic relationship. Even Bök initially configured the project in parasitic terms: "In this experiment, I propose to address some of the sociological implications of biotechnology by manufacturing a 'xenotext' — a beautiful, anomalous poem, whose 'alien words' might subsist, like a harmless parasite, inside the cell of another life-form."[35] Bök was (at least in 2008) engineering the poem with the scientist Stuart Kauffman so that "books of the future may no longer take on the form of codices, scrolls, or tablets, but instead they may become integrated into the very life of their readers."[36] In this way, *The Xenotext Experiment* strives to 'infect' the language of genetics with the 'poetic vectors' of its own discourse, doing so in order to extend poetry itself beyond the formal limits of the book."[37] The enciphered alphabet that Bök develops makes use of the basic communicational elements of

---

34   Bök used this gendered dynamic to describe his project in interview with Jamie Condliffe in *NewScientist* from May of 2011: Jamie Condliffe, "Cryptic poetry written in a microbe's DNA," *NewScientist,* May 4, 2011, https://www.newscientist.com/blogs/culturelab/2011/05/christian-boks-dynamic-dna-poetry.html.

35   Christian Bök, "The Xenotext Experiment," *SCRIPTed* 5 (2008): 228–31, at 229.

36   Bök, "The Xenotext Experiment," 230.

37   Ibid., 230.

DNA with its available vocabulary of *A* (Adenine), *C* (Cytosine), *G* (Guanine), and *T* (Thymine), which are the nucleotides that code for DNA, in order to create a constrained lexicon that can provide the available words for the poem. Bök has already written the poem that that he will embed and has reverse engineered the poem that the bacterium will produce in response. He has (as of 2017) successfully embedded the poem-parasite in E. coli, but the project has yet to be successful in D. radiodurans. E. coli lacks the resilience of D. radiodurans and Bök wants his poetry to be everlasting.

What if the importance of Bök's project is not to be found in the authorial goal of an embedded parasite-poem into a host-bacterium that results in the host's stammering and pre-programmed response, but rather in the implications that his project has for revealing our own language-parasite(s)? What if the human species stand in for D. radiodurans and the poem that the bacterium must utter is really what we call a "self?" Who has embedded this "self-poem" and how can we begin to see the parasite for what it really is? D. radiodurans does not know that the poem that it will utter is anything except the natural code of its own intrinsic functioning — its own organic autopoiesis and not an embedded and preprogrammed Bökian poiesis. What if our own "selves" are the results not of autopoiesis, but poiesis? If this is true, then our "selves" are not the results of a self-organized Governor (an autopoietic code that masquerades as hegemonic discourse), but a Parasite that has entered from the outside (as poiesis).

Citing the Parasite's "Nature"

Sometimes a para-cite lives at a para-site. The "para-cite" is my term for the ways in which scholars use existing texts as hosts and feed off them in order to produce their own scholarship. The very notion of citation is intrinsically parasitical. In the best conditions, citation is modeled after a symbiont more than a parasite, but often citation connotes a parasitic relationship. The forcible binarisms of the Governor negate or repress the alienation that instates the internal order of the host-parasite dynam-ic. Necessarily alienating, the experience of housing a parasite for the host renders the host as an alien to her, his, or their own body and selfhood. In this case, Marx's philosophy will assist in understanding the parasitic nature of capitalism and the ways in which capitalism engenders a profound sense of alienation and how — in traditional communist models — the bourgeoisie parasites the proletariat-host.

Marx draws a dividing line between mind and nature and suggests that there is something in "Man" that is intrinsically "not-nature": "alienated labour alienate[s] (1) nature from man, and (2) man from himself, his own active function, his vital activity."[38] This act of alienation produces a supplement to and in the subject — an other space that the subject occupies, a para-site to the other site — and this dual experience of the supplement and its resultant alienation makes the subject into a subject-of. The subject becomes a *subject-of alienation,* which is a cognitive or phenomenal site that can begin to apprehend the contours of the parasite. The transjected spaces that exist in between he-gemonic concepts such as "mind" and "nature" fractally fold in on each other and produce parasites, para-sites, and parasitic relations. In Michel Serres's *The Parasite* (1982), he understands the "parasite" to be a kind of interruption or noise that operates underneath reality ("parasite" means "noise" in French): "Theo-rem: noise gives rise to a new system, an order that is more com-plex than the simple chain."[39] The parasite-as-noise is productive of meaning and order. Throughout *The Parasite,* Serres refers to chaos theory and systems theory and the productive power of the interruption.[40] For Serres, the significance of the parasite

---

38 Karl Marx, *Selected Writings,* ed. David McLellan (Oxford: Oxford Univer-sity Press), 90.

39 Serres, *The Parasite,* 14.

40 See chaos theorist Ilya Prigogine and Isabelle Stengers's afterword to Serres's *Hermes* from 1982: Ilya Prigogine and Isabelle Stengers, "Postface: Dynam-ics from Leibniz to Lucretius," in Michel Serres, *Hermes: Literature, Science, Philosophy,* eds. Josué V. Harari and David F. Bell, 135–55 (Baltimore: Johns Hopkins University Press, 1982).

is directly related to the one that is parasited, which designates meaning-systems as either coherent or diffracted.

What Serres means by his notion of the "interrupted meal" features some similarities with Žižek's interpretation of "the voice" from *Enjoy Your Symptom!* (1992). Žižek discusses the parasiting nature of the Voice in relation to Chaplin's film *City Lights* (1931): "the disruptive power of the voice, of the fact that the voice functions as a foreign body, as a kind of parasite introducing a radical split: the advent of the Word throws the human animal off balance and makes of him a ridiculous, impotent figure, gesticulating and striving desperately for a lost balance."[41] The parasite inside language produces, through its disruptions and interruptions, the various irruptions or ruptures of meaning or non-meaning. The noise in the communicational signal assists in the creation of meaning: a little bit of noise is needed for the emergence of meaning, while too much noise results in the non-meaningful. Sense becomes non-sense depending on the degree of noise in the signal.

The Voice, like the interrupted meal, is interruptive. Lacan claims that "the real" is that which wakes us from sleep — a jarring interruption that shakes us back into the world and leaves us with the raw sting of the uncanny. For both Serres and Žižek, the interruption has special significance: the sign of the interruption awakens the host to the deeper awareness of her, his, or their status as an infected being — as the house of a parasite. The interruptions that annoy us signify the world as a totality that is prone to diffractions. Interruptions activate a sense of the unreal or the surreal and give way to *unheimlich* experiences like "déjà vu."

Uncanny experiences take on the form of a parasite: the interruption is similar to the tapeworm that crawls up the throat to get at the salt that is placed on the tip of the tongue. In other words, the interruption reveals the underlying constructions of the Governor. The interruption reveals the concealed "ofs" that

---

41 Slavoj Žižek, *Enjoy Your Symptom!: Jacques Lacan in Hollywood and Out* (New York: Routledge, 2008), 3.

designate the subject-of as being "subject-of" instead of as a fully coherent subject. After the experience of the real passes — or after the parasite recedes after crawling to the tongue — the world progresses just as it did before. For phorontology, interruptions are notable events and should be harnessed because they point to the deeper proto-structure of the sites and the para-sites: interruptions point to the proto-structure of the language-parasite as being composed of a metafractal.

What is a "metafractal?" Is the term not redundant? Is the term "metafractal" somewhat akin to saying "fractalfractal?" In a sense, all fractals are fractalfractals, but a metafractal is different and it is a useful term for conceptualizing phorontology. Phorontology seeks to describe the structures and proto-structures that compose the parasite of language and the transjected subject-ofs that constitute contemporary being: this goal can only be achieved by understanding how the concept of the metafractal points to the self-similar and self-organizing principles of transjects, xenojects, subjects, objects, subject-ofs, Governors, Houses, sites, and para-sites.

The Parasite that Dewdney describes is both consciousness and language and it features the normalizing processes of sociocultural customs and rituals. The Governor becomes a Parasite depending on how the overall organismic structure of the House of the living language is configured at that point in time. Subject-ofs multiply because there are more subject positions available in hyperhistory than ever before; put differently, I would say that the subject-of is the *strange attractor of identity*. Subject-ofs are akin to the strange attractors of chaos theory in that they are the seemingly coherent structures that stabilize the chaotic and fractal patterns of social (macro) and psychic (micro) systems. Subject-ofs should not be thought of as Lacanian "quilting points"[42] because consciousness is not linear; on the contrary, consciousness is dynamic and metafractal. What

---

42 Jacques Lacan, *The Seminar of Jacques Lacan: Book III: The Psychoses 1955–1956*, ed. Jacques-Alain Miller, trans. Russell Grigg (New York: Norton, 1997), 268–70.

Lacan would call "quilting points," I would call the "ofs" of the metafractal: these "ofs" should not be thought of as "buttons," but rather as nonlinear and aperiodic variables that shift and morph in relation to certain proto-structural conditions and tendencies in the total system. The parasite is fractal.

Conceptually, the notion of the "subject-of" emerges from Louis Althusser's work in his essay "Reply to John Lewis." What Althusser calls "interpellation" is one possible term that designates the underlying parasite that hails you on the street corner, but of more interest for the purposes of phorontology is Althusser's assertion here: "there is no Subject (singular) of history," Althusser writes, "[a]nd I will go further: 'men' are not 'the subjects' *of* history."[43] If there is no singular subject of history and if men are not the subjects of history, then what is? Althusser argues that "history has 'subjects'; these subjects are obviously 'men'; 'men' are therefore, if not the Subject of history, at least *the subjects* of history."[44] Althusser sketches out how the agency of the sentence resides not in the concept of the word "subject" or the word "subjects," and not even in the word "history," but rather in the preposition "of." Apart from emphasizing the patriarchy, Althusser also emphasizes the "of": "But the fact that they are necessarily subjects does not make the agents of social-historical practices into the *subject* or *subjects* of history (in the philosophical sense of the term: *subject of*). The subject-agents are only active in history through the determination of the relations of production and reproduction."[45] This Marxist analysis usurps agency or power from history and its subjects and places agency in the hands of the "of," which here connotes the material means of production and reproduction. This "of" is an "of" that designates recursivity and feedback: as a preposition the word links other parts of speech together, but it also weaves the concepts of "subject" and "history" together as well.

---

43 Louis Althusser, *On Ideology,* trans. Ben Brewster (London: Verso, 2008), 134.
44 Ibid., 133.
45 Ibid., 135.

In an Althusserian context, the "subject" is "of" "history" and this linkage can be expressed in numerous ways so that each explication emphasizes the shifting power relations between each concept in different ways. However, what I mean by the term "subject-of" is different from what Althusser means by the term: in a phorontological praxis, the word "of" is not necessarily linked to the concept of "history," but can be linked to numerous, nonlinear concepts that permit the emergence of a "subject." Certainly, this "of" — or these "ofs" — would be partly related to the ideological and the historical or to the Lacanian notion of master signifiers,[46] but there would be other influences as well: social, cultural, familial, ancestral, mythological, personal, and unconscious. The importance of the seemingly simple preposition "of" in the concept "subject-of" is that the "of" is constantly shifting in relation to the complex interplay of self and environment or subject and object. However many linkages exist at any given time between the self and the environment would designate the totality of the "ofs" and these "ofs" would shift and die off for the emergence of new "ofs" as the autopoietic nature of the biological and linguistic organism degenerates and regenerates. As these "ofs" grow, live, and die over time, the overall proto-structure of the metafractal repeatedly transforms into different sites and para-sites. The variety of these "ofs" can be thought of as individual or particular parasites — parasites that para-site the subjective site — or they can be thought of in more banal terms; namely, these "ofs" can be thought of as cultural memes.

Operating on the Parasite

Richard Dawkins theorizes the *meme* as an intrinsically parasitic model of cultural transmission, going so far as to link cul-

---

46 Jacques Lacan, *The Seminar of Jacques Lacan: Book XVII: The Other Side of Psychoanalysis,* ed. Jacques-Alain Miller, trans. Russell Grigg (New York: Norton, 2007), 170.

tural transmission with genetic transmission.[47] Dawkins defines "meme" in the following way:

> "Mimeme" comes from a suitable Greek root, but I want a monosyllable that sounds a bit like "gene." I hope my classicist friends will forgive me if I abbreviate mimeme to *meme* […]. Examples of memes are tunes, ideas, catch-phrases, clothes fashions, ways of making pots or of building arches. […] [S]o memes propagate themselves in the meme pool by leaping from brain to brain via a process which, in the broad sense, can be called imitation.[48]

By linking cultural transmission with genetic transmission, Dawkins is unwittingly making an argument that is reliant on fractal self-similarity: he is claiming that the systemic habits of genes in some ways mirror the systemic habits of cultural memes. Dawkins affords greater speed to the evolution of memes than the evolution of genes and he links the speed of meme evolution to that of linguistic evolution: "Language seems to 'evolve' by non-genetic means, and at a rate which is orders of magnitude faster than genetic evolution."[49] The high speed of linguistic evolution is related to the speed of cultural evolution, thereby linking memes and language together in terms of their shared parasitic qualities. Dawkins understands memes in parasitic terms, such as when he claims that: "memes should be regarded as living structures, not just metaphorically but technically. When you plant a fertile meme in my mind you literally *parasitize* my brain, turning it into a vehicle for the meme's propagation in just the way that a virus may parasitize the genetic mechanism of a host cell."[50] Subjects sometimes parasitize objects and objects sometimes parasitize subjects, but the ontological importance of the parasite is rarely considered in this

---

47 Richard Dawkins, *The Selfish Gene* (Oxford: Oxford University Press, 2006), 189.
48 Ibid., 192.
49 Ibid., 189.
50 Ibid., 192. Emphasis added.

dynamic. Ontology and phenomenology have historically addressed some of the questions and sites of Being — particularly, the question or site of a *human theory of being-human,* but ontology and phenomenology falter in front of other, posthuman, inhuman, or nonhuman forms of Being. A different theory of Being is required to address what it means to be a nonhuman. Phorontology preliminarily addresses this niche and begins to theorize the nonhuman being of the parasite.

For this reason, the focus of contemporary philosophy should no longer be on subjects or objects, but rather on transjects. Philosophical and material parasites are all *transjects* — they are transjected. The subject-of is a predominantly human instance of a *transject,* but there are other nonhuman, posthuman, and inhuman forms of transjects as well. The parasite is neither subject nor object, but a transject, which is a new ontological category that exists in between humanist subjects and nonhuman objects. The subject-of is the humanist face of the transject, but it is only one entification of the transject among many others; in other words, the subject-of is the parasitized instance of the subject in the same way that the subject-of parasitizes the transject.

Language and culture invade from an outside and infect the subject and render that subject into a subject-of. From a phorontological perspective, consciousness or sentience are likely the results of an "accident" or "mutation" that randomly occurred by virtue of an initial mutation — a mutation that manifests as the signature of the meme-parasite as it fights for neurological real estate. Dawkins situates the meme in aggressive terms: "If a meme is to dominate the attention of a human brain, it must do so at the expense of 'rival' memes. Other commodities for which memes compete are radio and television time, billboard space, newspaper column-inches, and library shelf-space."[51] If the language-parasite and the resultant subject-of are the results of an initial mutation that became passed on through natural selection and evolution, then that mutation must have been beneficial enough to outweigh the negative qualities of a mutation:

---

51   Ibid., 197.

"Almost all genetic side-effects are bad, and a new mutation will normally spread only if its bad effects are outweighed by its good effects. [...] In spite of its deleterious side-effects, if a segregation distorter arises by mutation it will surely tend to spread through the population."[52] The subject-of experiences sentience or self-awareness as the result of an invasive language-parasite that enters the subject-of from the outside and constructs that outside as an "outside." The "outside" becomes differently charged in the subject-of as the incursions of the symbolic order as exteriority affect the overall functionality and stability of the imaginarily coherent "subject." The outside parasitizes the subject and creates sentience out of the various "ofs" that virally proliferate inside lived experience. The mutations that permitted the dominance of the language-parasite have contributed to historically determinant hegemonies and realities. These "hegemonies" and "realities" have become concretized in human history by the replicative efficiency of memes; or, as Dawkins writes:

When we die there are two things we can leave behind us: genes and memes. We were built as gene machines, created to pass on our genes. But that aspect of us will be forgotten in three generations. Your child, even your grandchild, may bear a resemblance to you, perhaps in facial features, in a talent for music, in the colour of her hair. But as each generation passes, the contribution of your genes is halved. [...] But if you contribute to the world's culture, if you have a good idea, compose a tune, invent a sparking plug, write a poem, it may live on, intact, long after your genes have dissolved in the common pool. Socrates may or may not have a gene or two alive in the world today, as G.C. Williams has remarked, but who cares? The meme-complexes of Socrates, Leonardo, Copernicus and Marconi are still going strong.[53]

---

52 Ibid., 237.
53 Ibid., 199.

When a meme is internalized — consciously or unconscious-ly — it parasitizes a site of the subject-of; put differently, the in-ternalized meme becomes another "of" in the overall sitings and para-sitings of the metafractal.

If the sources discussed in this chapter point to a real pan-demic — a normalized pandemic that describes the hegemonic constitution of "normalcy" itself — then why should we care about it? Why would we need a logic of operation or treatment for a state of selfhood that is the standard ontological experience of "being-human?" If we begin to consider the normal function-ality of human sentience as being prone to parasitic infection, or as being the direct result of a parasitic infection, then we begin to theorize different avenues of subjective experience and more capacious alternatives to ontology. The question of "what is be-ing?" is a question (with already proposed and yet un-thought answers) that can be broadened by considering a phorontology instead of an ontology or a transject instead of a subject or an object. An acknowledgement of this pandemic will open new pathways for existence. However, whether or not the parasite *can* be operated on is likely a question that is best left to 'pata-physicians and the most daring philo-fiction detectives.

The Meta-site

SUBJECT-OFS ARE STRUCTURED BY PATTERNS of repetition and replication because *the future site* motivates the present and retroactively codes its existence as nonexistent or as "presently nonexistent." The future site is held away from the subject-of because it is structured on the basis of a "promise." The future site vacillates between being either a *para* or a *meta* singularity that oscillates due to indefinite feedback. The present site, on the other hand, is a site of constraint and the only escape from this constraint is the future site. The specific constraint — whatever that constraint may be — transforms the site into a *self* and outlines the borders of subjectivity in order to ensure that the self is always partial — never "full" or "total." The perceptual illusion of wholeness in the self is a simulation created by the parasite of constraint where the self remains an illusion or dream of atomism — a dream of a sovereign, nomadic existence. The self is "atomic" only insofar as it creates a perception of singularity; however, in the same way that the electron acts as both a wave and a particle, the atomic self is both particular and sited as a continuum. On the one hand, the "self" becomes a singularity when focalized as the local site of a subject-of, but, on the other hand, the subject-of becomes a continuum when that subject-of is effaced and misrecognized as a subject or self. These distinct states are complementary, but not necessarily simultaneous.

The future site prospectively defines the "play" or fuzziness of the present constraint. However, this "prospective definition" is also a retroactive siting of the imagination because the future site promises that the present site of constraint can be altered by a supplement (such as a dream or a goal) that can accommodate the overall structure of the intrinsic fractality of sites. The subject-of is a concept that denotes the underlying fractality of the subjective site (which I call the metafractal). When one is subject-of a specific site or a constraint, then the atomism of the "self" becomes prone to a wide variety of exceptions or declinations: the subject-of is designated as a simulated "whole" in relation to the various supplements that are made possible by the potential of the constraint.

The notion of a constraint is dictated by what Lucretius calls the *clinamen atomorum* (or the "atomic swerve").[1] Democritus argues that atoms fall downward in a never-ending waterfall, but it is Lucretius — after Epicurus — who theorizes the swerve that is produced by atomic collisions. According to Lucretius, when atoms collide they produce a swerve and this swerve is what permits the emergence of natural things. Sites function in similar ways. The site, as every future site or every prefixed site, is given form by the particular constraint — a constraint that is itself dictated by the associations of the subject-of and the unexpected declinations of the *clinamen*. The *clinamen* is, in this sense, the "hope" that is offered by a future site. The present has no intrinsic promise because the future site offers compensation for the present site; in other words, the existential "promise" is only provisionally existent in the present due to what the future site provides. This model creates a structure that is predicated on retroversion, feedback, and recursivity — this model presents sites as locales that repeat, circulate, and navigate the "host" through an environment. Sites are not chronologically specific, but are dependent on the *clinamen* (or a type of *clinamen*) for metamorphosis or fantasy.

Combining the notion of the subject with that of the atom would allow us to ask about the quanta of the self: is this quanta a Cartesian homunculus? If there is a subjective atom, then "it

1   See Lucretius, *On the Nature of Things: De rerum natura,* ed. and trans. Anthony M. Esolen (Baltimore: The Johns Hopkins University Press, 1995), II: 217–29 (or page 63).

has a real field *elsewhere, another* assignable site."[2] When every site is destroyed by the repressive regimes and despotic powers of a dystopic nightmare, then where can the subject flee? Is there a site that remains for this potential subject without "country?" We need a theory of the subject that is free from all ideological attachments — from all of the "ofs." Ideology functions as a corrective salve for a damaged site: where the subject fails, ideology-sites impose new systems of delimitation in which the "lost" subject can be re-mythologized within a new operative regime.

A historical moment is an unfixed site, but the language used to speak about that historical moment is unflinching and firm. What is called "history" is merely one palimpsestic-site among others in a total narrative-fractal. This narrative and historical situation leads me to call for a *militant grammatology* or a *guerrilla phorontology* that can address the fallibility of these damaged sites. The textual pathway of the Derridean trace is non-agential[3] because there is no militant impulse in Derridean grammatology. What could be called the "intentional trace" can be considered the *clinamen* that inaugurates order and structure within the chaos of the material world. The *clinamen* conceptually traces the collisions that occur within any metastasizing system: the atomic collisions that produce the Lucretian swerve are the events that inaugurate the multiple from the singular. The atom is never singular *stricto sensu,* but only one complex assemblage among many others.

Thresholds of collapse temporarily structure shapes and forms as "coherent" entities. What is needed to theorize this dynamic is a new theory of Form combined with an understanding of complexity theory: this new theory would require that every *form* and *structure* is dependent on the ontological count of that structure. The level of magnification would then dictate the manner in which that structure gets counted: if we are Deleuzoguattarians and choose to count to the molecular or the molar, then that decision (or de-scission) would deter-

---

2   Derrida, *Of Grammatology,* 60.
3   Ibid., 61.

mine the ontological result of that structure. For this reason, I insist that ontology is *threshold specific*. If ontology is threshold specific, then any "structure" is only "whole" in relation to its own dimensions and intrinsic geometries: if that structure were to be removed from its present state, then it would rapidly lose its manifest concreteness and dissipate into pure nothingness. Ontology is only "ontological" if entropy is also present in the overall system because entropy dictates the temporality and dimensional coherence of a subjective-structure. Writing as the representation of an ontology is also bound within laws of time and energy. Writing requires the medium of a writer or robot to function; otherwise that same writing would remain virtual. This writing that would include the graphematic and the phonematic is *situated* and *sited* in a space. Space partly becomes a "place" when it is occupied by the positionality of a mark or singularity. It is here that Foucault 'pataphysically combines with Derrida.

Foucault writes about the heterotopia, which is an "other space," as a specific site of liminal escape that is operative in modernity: "The great obsession of the nineteenth century was, as we know, history […]. The present epoch will perhaps be above all the epoch of space. We are in the epoch of simultaneity: we are in the epoch of juxtaposition, the epoch of the near and far, of the side-by-side, of the dispersed."[4] History occupies a virtual space that is made actual in its tracings: "history" is actualized in the carvings that decorate buttressed ceilings, in hieroglyphic records, or in the fossilized sediment of species long extinct.

Foucault writes that heterotopias are spaces of fossilized history: "there are heterotopias of indefinitely accumulating time, for example museums and libraries. Museums and libraries have become heterotopias in which time never stops building up and topping its own summit."[5] However, the library-heterotopia does not accumulate towards any final phase because hetero-

---

4   Michel Foucault, "Of Other Spaces," trans. Jay Miskowiec, *Diacritics* 16, no. 1 (1986): 22–27, at 22.
5   Ibid., 26.

topias are temporary sites of social alterity. Heterotopias do not maintain cohesiveness indefinitely throughout history: no matter the mortar or cement used in their construction, they are prone to the erasure of history and, furthermore, to the dispersive affects of entropy. Heterotopic spaces are anthills of Euclidean architecture that rupture, deteriorate, decay, and are re-built in order to house the future icons of an inward-looking civilization. The importance of heterotopias can be found in their impermanence: they are spaces that are subject to the dissolution of history while acting as the escape valves for a marginalized social order. The pyramids will never be heterotopic, while a rave venue may well be. However, a heterotopia is a space of alterity only in relation to the normative codes of society so that such a site is dependent on the *potential* populace that may one day populate it.

The dream of the heterotopia is the dream of an outside of the outside — the dream of a space that is exterior to all entropic deterioration. The ravages of time do not affect the heterotopia because it occupies an eternal present. Heterotopias dissipate and shift in the forced metamorphosis of entropy while remaining *in potentia,* but the postmortem emergence of hyperhistory has changed the potentiality of the heterotopia. For example, hyperhistory is de-sited where history is sited: history is sited in churches and ruins, while hyperhistory is de-sited in the simultaneity of historical multiplicity and the negation of the possibility of the archive. Hyperhistory consumes previous histories and exhumes these histories as gifts of futurity. Consumption should be understood here to mean both "theft" and "gift." Any form of consumption steals agency in that the consumed-object's totality is appropriated for the coherency of another object, while still remaining a gift for that initial object's claims of community. The consumed object is networked during the act of consumption. Consumption is therefore the consummation of a theft and a gift and is, in hyperhistorical terms, epitomized by the act of cannibalism.

Cannibalism can be considered one of the current phases of conceptual writing and avant-garde literary experimentation:

"cannibalism" denotes the appropriation or re-appropriation of prior texts within a "new" mode or gift that steals the inexistence of an "original." Baudrillard's theory of "simulation" cannibalizes the notion of the origin;[6] in other words, the original icon is eaten during the totemic meal. "Cannibalism" becomes a rhetorical tool deployed by colonialism after Christopher Columbus coins the term "cannibal" from the Caribs who were the cannibalistic tribe at war with the Arowaks.[7] Cannibalism depicts a basic mode of modern consumption as the tapeworm societies curl inside the hegemonic host.

In Homer's *The Odyssey* (c. 8th century BCE), the Cyclops Polyphemus and the Lestrygonians (a tribe of giant cannibals) eat Odysseus's men. A site is differently coded when feeding occurs within it. The heterotopia is a site of escape from society whereas the sites of the cycloptic and Lestrygonian meals are "different spaces" that are different not because they are "exterior" to society, but because they occur at an "interior" of an entirely different society. Odysseus and his men leave the formal sites of their homeland and enter into the other-sites of the Cyclops and Lestrygonians: these sites are then coded as inclusive to cycloptic and Lestrygonian society. The *nostos* or homecoming of Odysseus occurs by virtue of a recognition of the memory of hunger: Odysseus recognizes the site of his home because of his sexual hunger. Desire is not only predicated on a form of lack, but also, on the presence of hunger and on the pleasure that is derived from feeding.

6   Baudrillard, *Simulacra and Simulation,* 3–7.

7   A good source for the history of cannibalism (that also addresses colonialism and Columbus), see Bill Schutt's *Cannibalism: A Perfectly Natural History* (Chapel Hill: Algonquin Books, 2017). Also of interest for this topic is: Jeff Berglund's *Cannibal Fictions: American Explorations of Colonialism, Race, Gender, and Sexuality* (Madison: University of Wisconsin Press, 2006).

Parasite Semiotics

The agency of alterity locates the beginning of an undecidable dialectic between *author* and *other*. Otherness invites authorship because otherness para-sites the profound distance between the body, its hungers, and the exterior world. The cannibal is like a parasite who is an Other and also an Author. These terms combine to become an *auther*, which I consider to be an agential category of alterity in which forms of otherness are authorized into a new para-site — a para-site that is reconfigured as a site. The term "auther" names a specific strand of the subject-of that designates the authority or the power of the other to inscribe sites and para-sites.

Parasites are always in the process of homecoming. Odysseus returns home to Penelope and sees that countless suitors have attempted to "implant" themselves in his marriage bed. Penelope is akin to the anglerfish of the Ceratiidae variety in which the males of the species burrow within the body of the female and parasitically live off her body. The homecoming is rendered parasitic because Odysseus returns under the mistaken impression that he is singular in his status as "male" or "husband." He returns home to engage in a battle of masculinity, which can be understood as a battle of parasites. Penelope is an anglerfish who weaves a net that confines her parasite-suitors and it is only through the act of *angeln* (or fishing) that allows Penelope to weave a suitable burial shroud.

A *parasite semiotics* is required to understand the transition of an author to an auther. The term "auther" denotes a parasitized subject position that weaves in relation to a once externalized, but now internalized influence — an influence that arrives from before and beyond any subject. The parasite of constraint is responsible for the strict policing of the boundary between intimacy and extimacy. The parasite of constraint and its related language parasites pre-date human beings and require repetition and replication in order to survive.

The sign is originally a parasite in that it imbeds itself within speaking subjects. If you communicate, then you are living with a parasite. For phorontology, the central term of a para-site semiotics would be what Roman Jakobson calls "the phatic function."[8] Jakobson develops the term from Bronislaw Ma-linowski's theory of the "phatic."[9] The phatic function designates a social channel as being "active" — it forges the social bond be-tween addressor and addressee. However, the phatic is not nec-essarily related to the meaning of a signal, which would align it more with noise.

Noise is, for Serres, one of the central organizing forces in communication and it conceals (and is) a parasite. The message or channel is prone to the overcoded qualities of noise. It does not matter what the discourse is or the subtexts of the message are because the signal and the message can never contain the meaning *in toto.* The emergence of noise presents as the inter-rupture of the parasite; put differently, the phatic function be-comes emphatic because it contains a speaking that arrives from elsewhere. In a parasite semiotics, the communicational rela-tionship would always be triadic or multiple. There would never only be one speaker and one addressee because the parasites are already muttering within the signal itself.

A parasite semiotics that highlights the underlying noisi-ness of the phatic also activates Thomas Sebeok's biosemiotic and zoosemiotic theories of communication.[10] If the signal is not dyadic, but triadic or multiple, then the signal becomes fractal — a fractal-message that is transmitted through a fractal-environment. By linking the phatic with Saussure's concept of the paragram[11] — which is a coded message that lurks within language itself — we can begin to situate the phatic and the para-

8   See Roman Jakobson, "Closing Statement: Linguistics and Poetics," *Style in Language,* ed. Thomas Sebeok, 350–77 (Cambridge: MIT Press, 1960).
9   Ibid., 355.
10 See Thomas A. Sebeok, *Perspectives in Zoosemiotics* (The Hague: Mouton de Gruyter, 1972).
11 Jean Starobinski compiles some of Saussure's work on the paragram in: *Words upon Words: The Anagrams of Ferdinand de Saussure,* trans. Olivia Emmet (New Haven: Yale University Press, 1979). Also, see my essay on this topic: "Cage's Mesostics and Saussure's Paragrams as Love Letters," *Post-modern Culture* 22, no. 2 (2012), n.p.

gram as proto-structural or as presentational representatives of language's deep structure. In this approach, the signal becomes a multiplicity that is spoken by the parasites of language and is recorded through the graphematic or phonematic marks of the paragram. The parasite's message is coded and imbedded within language itself, but its message can be read in paragrams.

Saussure hunted for names — often the names of gods — in Vedic hymns and Saturnian verse, but he abandoned this research when he realized that these names appeared to be the random patterns of a living language. A parasite semiotics, on the other hand, would reject Saussure's wish to locate authorial intention and would insist instead that these names, words, and messages were knowingly encoded, but not by writers or authors; on the contrary, the paragrams would be "knowingly" encoded by language itself. If language is configured as an emergent structure that contains certain features and properties that self-organize in manners that are similar to the emergent properties found in nature, then the secret codes within language would be similarly emergent. The paragram could be considered a chance-based signal that emanates from language; or, even further, the paragram could be considered the *voice* of the parasite. Saussure recognizes the paranoid implications of his own paragrammic search, which suggests that language may be working independently of us.

This phorontological approach does not afford vitality to something nonexistent; on the contrary, a parasite semiotics simply suggests that there are countless codes that are present around and within the speaking subject at all times. These codes function as our interface with exteriorities, but, all the while, these codes also pre-date our own subjective emergence as self-reflexive beings — as subjects-of. Steve McCaffery argues that "paragrams are linguistically elusive forces because invisible but at the same time intensely unavoidable. Prigogine would note the paragram as introducing nonlinear complexities and disequilibria into seemingly stable, linear structures, provoking crisis within any closed semantic economy, simultaneously engendering meaning eruptively and fortuitously but also turning unitary meaning against itself."[12] The paragram is an eruptive and elusive force that operates within language: it structures the nominational efficiency of language while also signaling the various ruptures and interruptures of any semantic structure. As the voice of the parasite, the paragram organizes communicational strands while evidencing the loss and fracture of information. The paragram is not the same as noise because it permits the coherency of noise. The paragram is therefore the coalescent message that can be created from the diffusion and nonsense of noise. Perhaps surprisingly, the paragram is a message that is hidden within the noise of the signal as the agential function of language or as the voice of the parasite.

McCaffery insists that Saussure

> detects in all these works a persistently recurring group of phonemes that combined to form echoes of important words. In the *De rerum natura* of Lucretius, Saussure found extended multiple anagrams of the name APHRODITE. Implicit in this research is the curious nonphenomenal status of the paragram, that virtuality of any letter or phoneme to form semantic aggregates inaccessible to normal habits of readings. [...] [I]t's the unavoidable presence of the paragram — as a protosemantic force in all writing — that contaminates the notion of an ideal, unitary meaning and thereby counters the supposition that words can fix or stabilize in closure.[13]

Language is then not a system that stabilizes in closure; quite the contrary, language is a nonlinear and chaotic system that becomes coherent in relation to the disequilibria of noise and the loss of meaning. Nietzsche would likely respond to Saussure's paragram search in the following manner: "kleine vorlaute Burschen sehen wir mit den Römern umgehen, als wären diese ihresgleichen: und in den Überresten griechischer Dichter wüh-

---

12 Steve McCaffery, *Prior to Meaning: The Protosemantic and Poetics* (Evanston: Northwestern University Press, 2001), 13.

13 Ibid., 196.

len und graben sie, als ob auch diese *corpora* für ihre Sektion be-
reitlägen und *vilia* wären, was ihre eignen literarischen *corpora*
sein mögen" (We see small pushy young men associating with
the Romans as if they were their equals. They rummage around
and dig away in the remnants of the Greek poets, as if even these
were *corpora* [bodies] ready for their post-mortem examination
and were as *vilia* [vile] as their own literary *corpora* might be).[14]
Saussure rummages through the body of Lucretius and searches
within his *corpora* for the paragrammic remnants of the word
and name "Aphrodite." Saussure engages in a postmortem on
the Lucretian corpus: he digs through it for the parasite that au-
thored Lucretius's insights in *De rerum natura*. The paragram
is like a parasitic *clinamen* that lurks within language's status as
an emergent and aperiodic system. For this reason, I claim that
the next stage in the history of criticism — after postmodernism
and posthumanism — is *postmortemism*. The author has died
and is lying on the gurney, decomposing.

Contemporary writers, critics, and poets have cut up the author's corpse and corpus and dig around her, his, or their insides. Writing explodes in the evanescence of its temporality: in
the age of hyperhistory writing halts in favor of its excavations.
Why? Because writing is no longer about typing, but about re-
organizing older archives, corpuses, and oeuvres. This situation
is what we find in the strategies of "conceptual writing" — the
avant-garde movement spearheaded by Kenneth Goldsmith,
Christian Bök, Darren Wershler, and Vanessa Place. A body of
work is now a material body that is waiting to be parasited, har-
vested, and dissected.

Consider Wershler's conceptual project *the tapeworm foundry* (2000): it is a poetry book that collects a variety of different experimental book proposals into one long sentence. Every
book proposal is separated by the word "andor" so that the surrounding text proliferates like a string of tapeworms that circle

---

14 Friedrich Nietzsche, "Vom Nutzen und Nachteil der Historie Für das Leben," *Werke in Drei Bänden: Erster Band*, 209–85 (Munich: Carl Hanser
Verlag, 1954), 241. My translation.

around the intestine of writing. Here are two examples of Wershler's "tapeworms":

> andor point out that super mario world is actually a complex digital allegory for the writings of terence mckenna andor pen a treatise for andre breton and philippe soupault in which you discuss the magnetic fields emitted by each vowel when it attracts the surrounding consonants like iron filings and then note that sometimes the letter y emanates a magnetism of its own.[15]

As a movement, conceptual writing celebrates textual experiments that emphasize a thinkership more than a readership so that the decision to write becomes a de-scission that is made upon a previous body. The postmortem age is writ large on the surface of our new inscriptions.

The parasites rage inside the author. Postmortemism occurs at the cataclysmic apotheosis of the spectacle — during the idealized moment of an apocalyptic reverie or climax. Nietzsche asks, regarding the end-of-the-world: "Steckt nicht vielmehr in diesem lähmenden Glauben an eine bereits abwelkende Menschheit das Mißverständnis einer, vom Mittelalter her vererbten, christlich theologischen Vorstellung, der Gedanke an das nahe Weltende, an das bänglich erwartete Gericht?" (Is it not much more the case that in this paralyzing belief in an already faded humanity there sticks the misunderstanding of an idea of Christian theology inherited from the Middle Ages, the idea of the imminent end of the world, of the nervously awaited judgment?).[16] Various "ends of history" have lead to our postmortem era: Alexandre Koyré and Alexandre Kojève both read Hegelian philosophy through the notion of an end of history (Koyré through the "owl of Minerva" and Kojève through the

---

15 Darren Wershler-Henry, *the tapeworm foundry: andor the dangerous prevalence of imagination* (Toronto: Anansi, 2000), n.p.

16 Nietzsche, "Vom Nutzen und Nachteil der Historie Für das Leben," 259. My translation.

figure of Napolean)[17]; much later, Francis Fukuyama locates the end of history in the liberal state.[18] Another figure of interest here would be Georges Bataille who considered the early twentieth century to be another "end of history" — a historical moment shockingly similar to Hegel's own.

According to Kojève, Hegel thought that the end of history would arrive in 1806, but, at one point, Kojève felt that Stalin — as opposed to Napolean — would trigger the end of history;[19] however, after World War II, Kojève once again agrees with Hegel. Bataille begins the publication *Acéphale* (that ran from 1936–1939) in order to propose his own posthuman solution to the end of history:[20] what Bataille calls *acéphalité* (or "headlessness") would function as an early postmortem for the Enlightenment project. In the concept of "headlessness," Bataille situates a form of agency that could lead to new sexual plenitudes and novel limit experiences.

The notion of the "end of the world" retroactively organizes the temporality of the language parasites. Like the scene in Ridley Scott's *Alien* (1979) where the parasitic alien explodes from Kane's chest, the parasite will postdate us and retroactively code us as already fallen. Why? We are fallen because Homo sapiens are a kind of superorganism. A superorganism is a totality composed of countless parts like an ant colony or a beehive.[21] The ant colony can move as *one body,* but it is composed of countless little bodies. The parasite exists as a pure multiplicity because it is always living within or alongside: therefore it cannot be counted as One. The One of any superorganism is only ever an imaginary One because the superorganism is simultane-

17 Elisabeth Roudinesco, *Jacques Lacan: An Outline of a Life and a History of a System of Thought,* trans. Barbara Bray (Cambridge: Polity, 2005), 97 and 101.
18 Francis Fukuyama, *The End of History and the Last Man* (New York: Free Press, 2006), xi.
19 Roudinesco, *Jacques Lacan,* 102.
20 Ibid., 131.
21 See William Morton Wheeler, "The Ant-Colony as an Organism," *The Journal of Morphology* 22, no. 2 (1911), 307–25, and his book *The Social Insects, Their Origin and Evolution* (New York: Harcourt Brace, 1928).

ously singular and multiple: a superorganism is an assemblage or aggregate of smaller beings. The parasite exists within a site, which is the site of the host and this site is signified by its being a temporary space, but it is a site more than a territory because it manifests inside another site. A site is, to that end, not strictly geographical or geological, but embodied; for this reason, a site can potentially be an abstract idea such as "love" or a material entity like a friend.

Phorontology offers a modality of speaking about entities or objects — entities or objects that are inside other entities and objects — while simultaneously acknowledging the ontological count of the beings in the noted relation. Not only is phorontology concerned with the siting of objects, subjects, transjects, properties, and qualities, but it is also concerned with the situations that result from these sites. On the one hand, a site is similar to a mathematical set that incorporates items and objects such as numbers as members; however, on the other hand, every site contains corresponding parasites — parasites that para-site the earlier site and render it fractal. In this situation, whole numbers fail and fractions emerge. A phorontological understanding of set theory would consider the parasite to be a para-site within a site, which could also be called a realist *manifestation* of the paradox of the set of all sets.

Phorontology is not only realist in its approach to groups, communities, and boundaries, but it also presents a mode of thought that is post-deconstructive: phorontology levels the ground of the original construction and attempts to locate the site that permitted the construction. This claim does not erase cornerstones; instead, phorontology asserts that an originary locale exists, but remains imaginary. This locale or site would be causative because it remains non-coded: it pre-codes or post-codes the construction. The site or locale would exist either before the construction occurs or after the deconstruction has leveled the text. A site is a word, place, or thing; therefore, a site is usually, in a linguistic context, nounal. However, a site also *conveys a situation* to a subject-of and this situation activates various verb-forms. That being said, phorontology is not interested in the agency of the verb-form, but in the object-status of the verb form. Every verb is potentially an object when it is either stationary or imaginary. The site is therefore a space that *derecognizes* formerly recognized and normalized codes. To that end, phorontology proceeds by the strategy of *derecognition*. An example of derecognition would be the ceaseless repetition of a word: when a word is constantly repeated or read, then it becomes unfamiliar to the speaker or reader. While every site is partly a space of derecognition, an experience of derecognition can be simulated through practiced repetition. Phorontology incorporates tactics of both postmortemism and spectaclysm because the derecognition of a word leads to that word's death: when a word becomes devoid of meaning it dies in the dimension of the semiotic. The act of derecognition initially leads to the demise of a word and then, inevitably, to the postmortem of that word.

Two illustrative examples of a proto-phorontological approach can be found in the poetry of Gertrude Stein (for modernism) and Kenneth Goldsmith (for late postmodernism or conceptualism). Both Stein and Goldsmith derecognize the word in drastically different ways, but both accomplish this task through the strategy of repetition. Derecognition is the end effect of repetition.

Stein's *The Making of Americans* (1925) is a 925-page "novel" in which Stein analyzes the genealogies and histories of the Dehning and Hersland families. The work could be considered Stein's response to the genealogies of a writer like Tolstoy, but the difference between Tolstoy's genealogies and Stein's can be found in Stein's use of repetition:

Any one has come to be a dead one. Any one has not come to be such a one to be a dead one. Many who are living have not come yet to be a dead one. Many who were living have come to be a dead one. Any one has come not to be a dead one. Any one has come to be a dead one. Any one has not come to be a dead one. Very many who have been living have not yet come to be dead ones. Very many are being living. Very many who were being living are not being living, have come to be dead ones. Many who came to be old ones came then to be dead ones. Many who came to be almost old ones came then to be dead ones.[22]

In 2012, the poet Holly Melgard composed a text that was derived from Stein's *The Making of Americans*. In Melgard's work every repetition found in Stein's original was excised so that Stein's primary mode of experiment becomes sieved through a non-repetitive re-write. To illustrate the extent of Stein's experiment with repetition one has only to look at the length of Melgard's shortened version: the non-repetitive text of *The Making of Americans* is 21 pages.

In *The Making of Americans,* Stein derecognizes not only certain words and phrases, but also entire swathes of the English language:

> He was interested in this thing something almost completely interested in this thing, he was sometimes almost completely interested in being certain that something would be happening, he was sometimes almost completely interested in being certain that something was going to be happening and then that thing was happening. He was almost completely clearly feeling being one being living. He was almost completely clearly feeling being one going on being living. He was not completely needing this thing being one going on being living. He was almost completely needing the thing being one being living. Some are ones needing being one succeeded in living. Some are ones not needing being one succeeded in living.[23]

Stein interrogates the *site* of genealogy, which is the site of language and she renders that site as strange and unfamiliar: she

---

22 Gertrude Stein, *The Making of Americans: Being a History of a Family's Progress* (London: Dalkey Archive, 2006).
23 Ibid., 879.

de-sites language and reveals the sites that lurk underneath the signs.

Kenneth Goldsmith, like Gertrude Stein, seeks to derecognize language, but his approach is different because, unlike Stein, he has no interest in the repetition of words and phrases that are placed in close proximity to one another. Goldsmith's use of the site of language is quite different because where Stein is interested in the derecognition of words and phrases, Goldsmith is interested in the derecognition of entire archives. Goldsmith is a conceptual poet who locates, within archives and previous texts, a hotbed of uncreative writing: he often plagiarizes and re-types another author's text exactly as it has already appeared. Goldsmith is essentially a robopoet or typist — a machine who records previous texts and makes these texts unfamiliar by altering their sites. Goldsmith occasionally alters texts, but he is more interested in directly re-writing previous texts, such as when he types out radio reports in *The Weather* (2005) or traffic reports in *Traffic* (2007).[24] By changing the material conditions of a text — such as by re-typing the text in a different context, or by publishing the text on different paper, or even by engaging in the labor of re-typing a text — Goldsmith, after Borges's Pierre Menard, effectively engages in a realist and materialist writing practice that de-sites or re-sites other textual-sites. Phorontology approaches sites through the material and realist conditions of their constructions so that each construction can be considered as either sited or de-sited. Goldsmith's (re)writings are, in this context, de-scissional and de-sited writing practices. By derecognizing an archive through its repetition, Goldsmith effectively de-sites the text and makes it derecognizable. The avant-garde experiments of writers like Goldsmith and Stein

---

24 Recently, Goldsmith's appropriative practice has entered politically problematic waters when, on March 13, 2015, at the Interrupt 3 conference at Brown University, he read the official autopsy report of Michael Brown, the black youth killed by police officer Darren Wilson in Ferguson, Missouri in August 2014. The outcry with which the piece was received emphasizes that the failure or success of any conceptual piece is reliant on the context surrounding that appropriative practice.

seek to derecognize the word, phrase, or archive in order to find a new non-meaningful meaning that is present within language: a paradoxically non-meaningful meaning that is inherently coded during the re-siting of a text within new material conditions and novel textual iterations.

The 'Patasite

Laruelle's Decisions: Non-Philosophy and Phorontology

I partly relate François Laruelle's non-philosophy to phorontology through his emphasis on the concept of "Decision." A
Decision encapsulates an essential act of cutting — a de-scission — that necessarily eliminates the breadth of virtual possibilities or the continua of thought and actualizes certain pathways
instead of others. Non-philosophy strives to be non-Decisional
in that it attempts to actualize all virtual possibilities of thought
in order not to delimit a thought's breadth as either "good" or
"bad," but rather to present philosophy *qua* philosophy or a specific philosophy as consisting of a real continuum.

What I call a "site" connotes a fuzzy and non-Decided space:
a space that has not yet progressed through the various de-scissions that render a space into a place. A site is therefore not of
the world: it precedes the emergence of a "world" in a non-Decisional ecosystem that has denied any cut or strategies of cutting. Phorontology is therefore a speculative practice that resists
certain Decisions in an effort to, like non-philosophy, maintain
a virtuality of philosophy (or a cloning of philosophy). However,
the virtuality of philosophy remains un-actualized only insofar
as certain thoughts are, from an institutional and discursive perspective, more "philosophical" than others. I prefer the speculations of a philosophy that focuses on sites and para-sites that
exist outside of the human world. In a sense, speculative philosophies, like non-philosophy and speculative realism, are philosophical responses to movements such as quantum mechanics
and contemporary astronomy: quantum mechanics has dealt
with strange realities for over a hundred years while much of

continental philosophy has (until the emergence of speculative realism, object-oriented ontology, and the earlier Laruellean movement), remained locked in a mire of subjectivity and a linguistics of being (for much of the twentieth century). Phorontology is speculative because it emphasizes *both* the causative and the non-causative in that it points to a theoretically "pure" — i.e., non-Decided or non-desited — site; in other words, phorontology focuses on a site that exists prior to any construction. The space becomes a constructed-place when certain de-scissions are made actual, thereby separating geographies into territories.

Phorontology is speculative because it remains prior to or outside of certain Decisions. Phorontology is, to that end, both a speculative philosophy and also a linguistic branch of 'Pataphysics. 'Pataphysics mixes *metaphysics* and *paraphysics,* remaining interested in the beyond of metaphysics; i.e., 'Pataphysics focuses on the dimensionally anterior sites and para-sites of reality — or the 'patasites of reality, irreality, and surreality. What 'pataphysicians would call "ethernity" can be interpreted in similar terms as the virtual and non-Decisional continua of non-philosophical thought.

Speculative Metasentience

Phorontology prefers the speculative potential offered by the being of parasites because human consciousness is produced by a parasite-relationship: one of the first parasites of self-reflexive consciousness is language. Perhaps surprisingly, such speculation shares similarities with some strains of speculative fiction and hard science fiction: in July of 2004, the science fiction writer Peter Watts became interested in a bizarre article that was circulating through media outlets. The article reported that spontaneous bipedalism had occurred in a monkey after that monkey had survived a serious bout of the flu. Reporter Dan Waldman writes that:

Natasha, a 5-year-old black macaque at the Safari Park near Tel Aviv, began walking exclusively on her hind legs after a stomach ailment nearly killed her, zookeepers said [...]. Two weeks ago, Natasha and three other monkeys were diagnosed with severe stomach flu. At the zoo clinic, she slipped into critical condition [...]. After intensive treatment, Natasha's condition stabilized. When she was released from the clinic, Natasha began walking upright. "I've never seen or heard of this before," said Horowitz. "One possible explanation is brain damage from the illness," he said.[1]

On July 22, 2004, Peter Watts responded to this article in a blog post entitled: "Brain Damage. The Very Essence of Humanity." Watts speculates, regarding such a parasite-induced evolution, that

[b]ipedalism has been cited as the genesis of humanity. It freed us to use our hands, leading to increased manual dexterity, bigger brains, tool use, and global domination. But of all the theories I've ever seen put forth to explain why we started walking erect in the first place — nursing, thermoregulation, the need to see where the hell you were when the tall grass of the African savannah blocked your view — I don't recall anyone ever citing brain damage as the catalyst. Fellow Mammals, it don't get more ironic than that.[2]

What Watts calls "brain damage" could just as easily be called a "mutation" or "parasite" that alters the normative functionality of the overall machine, thereby reprogramming the machine so that it behaves in a different manner. Like the mind-controlling fungus Orphiocordyceps unilateralis — a parasite-fungus that grows out of an ant's head in order to use that ant's body like a remote-controlled robot — bipedalism can be considered

---

1   See http://www.nbcnews.com/id/5479501#.UxehNXmN1G4. The Wikipedia entry about the story can be found at http://en.wikipedia.org/wiki/Natasha_(monkey).
2   See http://www.rifters.com/real/newscrawl_2004.htm. Scroll down to the date posted.

a corollary of consciousness so that, speculatively speaking, self-awareness may be the result of a mind-controlling parasite.[3]

The fish parasite, Cymothoa exigua, is an isopod that takes up residence in fish gills. When it lives in fish gills it is male, but Cymothoa exigua is a protandric hermaphrodite, which means that it becomes a female later in its life cycle. At this point, the marine louse travels from the gills and takes up residence in the fish's mouth, clamping down overtop of the tongue and draining that organ's blood until it atrophies and falls off. Cymothoa exigua proceeds to function as the fish's tongue. At various points in the life cycle, other males from the gills travel to the mouth and mate with the female/tongue parasite in order to create future generations of Cymothoa. This isopod literally becomes the tongue of the fish. The *parasite speaks.*

Consciousness or subjectivity (defined here as an intelligent and sentient self-recursive system) may also be akin to Toxoplasma gondii infection, a parasite whose primary host is cats, but can be transmitted to humans and other mammals. Toxoplasma gondii is one of the world's most prevalent of parasites, infecting up to one third of the world's human population. In humans, the parasite seems to increase certain risk-taking behaviors, including a higher incidence of not looking both ways when crossing the street and sexual arousal when exposed to the smell of cat urine. Toxoplasma gondii is one of the most common chronic and unobstructive parasites — unless one suffers from the immunodeficiency that may result in toxoplasmosis — that many humans live with on a daily basis. Following Peter Watts's speculations regarding consciousness, sentience may well be one of the various benign parasites that we all live with everyday.

I have considered a variety of potential speculative parasites that may have contributed to consciousness and I have analyzed

---

3   Gary Shipley links parasitosis to suicidal ideation in *The Death of Conrad Unger* (2012). He focuses on the Orphiocordyceps unilateralis fungi and the hairworm. Shipley considers the suicidal thoughts of his friend Conrad Unger (and also Gérard de Nerval, Virginia Woolf, David Foster Wallace, and Ann Quin) as a kind of parasitic infection.

these "objects" as exterior influences (symbolic or real) that have written consciousness *après la lettre,* thereby denying any agency to "subjectivity" or being. These objects have included the fields of memetics, parasitology, Bök's *The Xenotext,* Dewdney's 'pataphysical poetics, the Gutenberg revolution, capitalism, consumption, the Saussurean paragram, conceptual writing, and the Lucretian *clinamen,* but each of these objects or fields can be summarized as encompassing one basic trait — namely, a certain degree of self-reflexivity.

Self-reflexivity is parasitic because it induces what I call "metasentience," which creates an other and makes that other operative within a psychic system or worldview. Peter Watts reads self-reflexivity as not only instating a self-other dyad or as creating a sentient multiplicity that involves feedback from an exterior world, but also as permitting such behaviors as "mooching." In an August 6, 2004 blog post entitled "The Secret of Sentience," Watts writes:

The secret of sentience, is … wait for it…

Mooching. If you can mooch, you're sentient.
No, bear with me here. This is brilliant. I'm not talking about an animal hanging out some place where he's learned there's food to be had. I'm talking about the active, premeditated mooch, the manipulation of moochee by moocher. I'm talking expectation and eye contact. When an organism simply shows up and waits for food to drop out of the sky, that's just operant conditioning. But when a sparrow with a brain the size of a lentil — basically, a hopping piece of feathered popcorn — actually looks you in the eye, and changes its behaviour based on what it sees there, we're talking something else again. When the expected food doesn't materialise, and the would-be moocher actually fixes you with a baleful bird stare and *scolds* you, we're talking something that has a *Theory of Mind.*

> Such a creature is not treating you as an inanimate object, he's treating you as a fellow autonomous agent with your own agenda.[4]

Phorontology does not only focus on the architectonics that are built upon a site or on the various inanimate objects that proliferate within a construction or place; instead, phorontology analyzes *agential transjects* — transjects that have become autonomous. If metasentience is partly the result of a parasite-evolution — an underlying mutation that has become normalized over time — then sentience is one instance of the parasite and the mooch is another. Watts's second example — in which a pigeon becomes associated with a "theory of mind" — emphasizes the parasitic nature of social organization. The social order is organized not only on the basis of hierarchies and deployments of power, but also on the mooching strategies that are prevalent within any strata of social communication.

The levels of parasites multiply: language is parasitic because it pre-dates us and outlines the lexical confines of our own speech and thought; metasentience is parasitic because its function is not predicated on the organism's survival; and communication contains not only noise in its messages, but also the social parasitism in which the addressor and addressee *want* something from each other. These agendas are intrinsically parasitic. I call this informatic dynamic the *symbi-ontic,* which is a concept that combines the notions of the symbiont and the ontic. The ontic is the philosophical category of *what there is*: it is a level-specific category of the ontological that focuses on a subject or object's real-status. A symbiont is an organism that must live alongside another in order to survive: examples include all organisms that live mutually, commensally, and parasitically; i.e., the lactobacilli that pervade human intestines, lichen, fleas, hermit crabs, etc. The *symbi-ontic* then would define the *real* manifestation of the ontic because nothing lives, exists, or *is* independently of

---

4 See http://www.rifters.com/real/newscrawl_2004.htm. Scroll down to the posting date.

itself. There is always a site or a host that functions as a categorical container for something else. The symbi-ontic can therefore be considered the set-theoretical combination of complexity theory and the ontic. The symbi-ontic conceptually approaches complex social systems as assemblages that exist within and *alongside* other groups. The symbi-ontic presents a fractal *picture* of social groups in which the possibility of a demarcation or a dividing line — a border where one object begins and another ends — is impossible, or at the very least, theoretically infinite and iterative.

The Parasite in Being

Vladimir *sh*Cherbak and Maxim Makukov make the argument that alien signals may be parasitically encoded within human DNA. They argue that because

> the actual scenario for the origin of terrestrial life is far from being settled, the proposal that it might have been seeded intentionally cannot be ruled out. A statistically strong intelligent-like 'signal' in the genetic code is then a testable consequence of such scenario. Here we show that the terrestrial code displays a thorough precision-type orderliness matching criteria to be considered an informational signal.[5]

The theory that terrestrial life is "seeded" by alien intelligences re-sites human beings as the parasites of alien hosts, or, because the symbi-ontic is multidirectional, the alien code would be the parasite that infects our DNA.

*sh*Cherbak and Makukov insist that an *alien signature* — a decidedly non-Derridean signature — remains hidden within DNA: "It is possible, at least in principle, to arrange a mapping that both conforms to functional requirements and harbors a

---

5   Vladimir I. *sh*Cherbak and Maxim A. Makukov, "The 'Wow! Signal' of the Terrestrial Genetic Code," accepted for publication in *Icarus,* arXiv: 1303.6739v1 (Sub. March 27, 2013), 1.

small message or a signature, allowed by 384-bits of informational capacity of the code."[6] Their argument relies on the *structure* of DNA and its resistance to change and mutation over large periods of cosmic history. This resistance to change situates DNA as a sort of cryptogram that requires an interpretive cipher: this "cipher" would be, for *sh*Cherbak and Makukov, the signature of an alien intelligence. The structure of DNA, they argue, suggests in a "statistically strong" manner that an "intelligent-like 'signal'" resides within "terrestrial genetic code."[7] Sounding very much like *sh*Cherbak and Makukov, extra-terrestrial paranoia also surfaces in Bök's *Xenotext* experiment: "aliens wishing to communicate with us might have already encoded messages in DNA, sending out legions of small, cheap envoys — self-maintaining, self-replicating machines that perpetuate their data over eons in the face of unknown hazards."[8] *sh*Cherbak and Makukov do not cite either Bök's experiment to embed a poem in a bacterium or Dewdney's 'pataphysical poetics that locates a parasite inside the Poet or Author. For Dewdney, the Author is not dead (as she or he is for Barthes), but only infected and controlled by a parasite intelligence. One reading would interpret Bök's project as situating human beings as the host or the alien to the parasited bacterium, but another reading would consider the bacterium itself as the host of the parasite-poem. In other words, the "host" can never be definitively located and neither can the "parasite": Hegel's master-slave dialectic transforms into the undecidable relationship of the site and the parasite. The relationship is no longer predicated on subjectivity or humanity: there is no lord or bondsman, but only a variety of different strata — objects, subjects, transjects, and anterior processes that are situated differently in relation to centralized attractors. Dewdney uses the following diagram to depict the parasite that lurks within the brain of every subject or author.

---

6   Ibid.
7   Ibid.
8   Bök, "The Xenotext Experiment," 228.

FIGURE 4: The Cerebral Cortex
Dominant Hemisphere

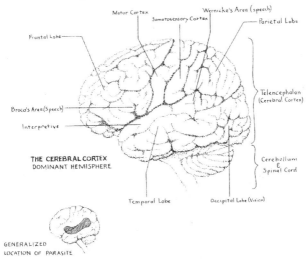

Fig. 1. Location of the Parasite (Dewdney, *Alter Sublime,* 89).

Unlike Dewdney, I do not claim that a "traditional" parasite lurks within the brain; that being said, I do argue that a parasite resides inside language and Being in order to organize subjectivity. This "parasite" is the base structure of an unconscious that is structured like a language. Giorgio Agamben also reads language as being parasitic, especially when he adds language to Foucault's list of apparatuses: "language itself, which is perhaps the most ancient of apparatuses — one in which thousands and thousands of years ago a primate inadvertently let himself be captured, probably without realizing the consequences that he was about to face."[9] By reading language as an apparatus, Agam-

---

9   Giorgio Agamben, *What Is an Apparatus? And Other Essays* (Stanford: Stanford University Press, 2009), 14.

ben situates language as a fundamental parasite that permits a "primate's" entry into the symbolic order.

The symbi-ontic is, properly speaking, a neologism that collides the *symbolic,* the *ontic,* and the *symbiont.* The symbi-ontic denotes the parasitic collapse of the symbolic associations of the various symbiontic relationships that structure all transjected creatures. The symbolic order preceded the first primate and existed before that primate entered into the parasitic field of the semiotic. First and foremost, *sentience is a sentence.* Sentience is a sentence because every sentence must be spoken or written; i.e., sentience is a concept that is transmitted into and through language. Put differently, "sentience" becomes sited or situated within a sentence. Language transmits sentience into a sentence, but only by virtue of already present locales of feedback and recursivity: when sentience is sited in a sentence, then *metasentience emerges.* Metasentience denotes a "face" of the subject-of that registers the symbi-ontic qualities of sentience.

As I mentioned earlier, Burroughs insists that "the word is now a virus,"[10] but this insight initially derives from his cut-up experiments with Brion Gysin in the 1960s. The cut-up is a formal and procedural textual experiment in which a text (or a variety of texts) are cut-up and permuted together, thereby producing a new text. Burroughs believed that cutting through "word lines" allowed the future to leak into the present. In Burroughs and Gysin's collaborative work *The Exterminator* (1961), the pair began to understand that language is a parasite-force that enters into and controls the human subject. Consider the following cut-up:

New York..Jan29 1960 Past Time — A German Virologist has succeeded in modifying the basic hereditary material of a virus in such a way as to be able to identify its effects on future generations..Perhaps the most significant step to date in deciphering The Language of Life. "Sooner or later this will lead to an understanding of the language of the virus which is the

10 Burroughs, *The Ticket That Exploded,* 49.

language of life." He said "The entire message of life is written in four letter words with our genes."[11]

Burroughs and Gysin discover messages in their experiments — they cut-up newspapers alongside Shakespeare, Rimbaud, and Burroughs's own massive "word hoard" manuscript — and discover, within the cut-ups, countless messages that uncannily align with Watts, Agamben, Chomsky, Dewdney, and Lacan's paranoid observations regarding language's parasitic self-awareness. Another cut-up reads: "According to the imminent scientists 'The message that is you' was written in virus left behind in shit and other junk abandoned by Space Tourists who took a look around and pulled out or did They?"[12] Despite the scientological resonance of this claim (Burroughs was interested in L. Ron Hubbard's scientology), I think that what is more important here is the structure and function of language. At some point in the life cycle of the language-system, language became aware of its own existence as a system. Another cut-up that points to this insight can be found in *The Exterminator*: "We can crack code write now. Doctor..It says: 'I am the Virus. I occupy Thee Host..I control your 'thoughts feelings and apparent sensory impressions'..Life can be written in Thee Sickness-Host.. What Virus Sends You MAN?..'"[13] Metasentient hosts contain an interiorized self that may be the result of a misrecognition of an exterior parasite that has reprogrammed the outside as a new "inside."

Recursivity is the basic structure of the Parasite. Subject-ofs and posthuman transjects suffer as infected beings: the first consideration of a posthuman phenomenology should state that *to be* means, first and foremost, *to be infected*. This infection marks the existence of our parasite guest. Being-in-time means being the host of an entity that is symbolic and exterior; in other

---

11 William Burroughs and Brion Gysin, *The Exterminator* (San Francisco: Dave Haselwood Books, 1967), 10.
12 Ibid., 25.
13 Ibid., 10.

words, the subject-of is a transject-symbiont that houses another transject-symbiont. Recurrence is essential to any consideration of postmortemism because the riposte of postmortemism can be found in the resurrection of the corpse lying on the gurney. Every corpus is revivified in postmortemism as everyone's Warholian fifteen minutes recur again and again: Nietzsche's *ewige Wiederkunft* (eternal recurrence) cycles through Vico's *storia ideale eterna* (ideal eternal history) and brings us into the twenty-first century.

Concepts of repetition are structured like a parasite: the parasite repeats a certain behavior that maintains the heredity and survival of the parasite. Language is, in this parasitic model, what Jameson would call a "structural void,"[14] which he relates to Lacan's *sujet supposé savoir* (the subject supposed to know) as an epistemological blank slate that acts as a structuring beacon within the chaotic semiotic field. The *sujet supposé savoir* is an entirely fictional siting of an imaginary persona within a space of epistemological plenitude: the phrase signifies the grounding of someone — typically an analyst — within a place, building, or framework of knowledge. Such a structural void depicts a site that can be cited as a place of knowledge that becomes seemingly stable when historicized (Jameson), schizophrenized (Deleuze and Guattari), deconstructed (Derrida), politicized (Marx, Gramsci), dialecticized (Hegel, Adorno), or queered (Butler, Wittig), (and there are many other thinkers and examples that could be added to this pitifully circumscribed list). Jameson argues that such a void operates in "the name of difference, flux, dissemination, and heterogeneity; Deleuze's conception of the schizophrenic text and Derridean deconstruction come to mind. If such perceptions are to be celebrated in their intensity, they must be accompanied by some initial appearance of continuity, some ideology of unification already in place,

---

14 Fredric Jameson, *Postmodernism: or, The Cultural Logic of Late Capitalism* (Durham: Duke University Press, 2005), 53.

which it is their mission to rebuke and shatter."[15] Such a field of knowledge becomes paradoxically stable when there is a nonexistent and yet stabilizing force. Following Lacan and Jameson, knowledge must be sited *somewhere.* To that end, the parasite is "real" because it situates the "host" as imaginary. The host does not exist because the very notion of a "host" is predicated on a concealed power differential. The parasite feeds on the host while that host lives at home.

In phorontology, dyadic, dualistic, or hegemonic distinctions are the unnecessary simplifications of complexity — complexity that includes transjects, segments, segmentations, and para-sites. To that end, phorontology disrupts the question of both human and animal: Agamben's historicization of the Greek distinction between *bios* (life as according to an individual or a group) and *zoē* ("bare life" that is common to men, animals, and gods)[16] is conceptually re-sited when viewed parasitically. Site/parasite and host/guest may appear to be structurally dyadic, but they do not *function as dyads* because, like Hegel's classic fable of the master and the slave, there is no stable site for power in any constructed binary.

From the perspective of *bios,* the parasite may be seen as something unpleasant, but from the perspective of *zoē* — a category that would encompass both the *site* and the *parasite* — a parasite is simply an entity that lives within or alongside another entity. However, phorontology discards the terms *bios* and *zoē* in favor of the symbi-ontic. The symbi-ontic is a term that displaces older categories such as "man" and "animal." A subcategory of the symbi-ontic — as the category of the transjected status of human and animal — could be called the ani-human. The phorontological term "*ani-human*" emphasizes the etymological basis of "animal "that derives from the Latin word *anima,* which means "breath" while neologistically maintaining both

---

15 Fredric Jameson, *The Political Unconscious: Narrative as a Socially Symbolic Act* (Ithaca: Cornell University Press, 1982), 53.

16 Giorgio Agamben, *Homo Sacer: Sovereign Power and Bare Life,* trans. Daniel Heller-Roazen (Palo Alto: Stanford University Press, 1998), 1.

the "human" within a philosophical transject-body. The distinction between "human" and "animal" becomes transjected in favor of a shared physiological, physical, and biological site (and situation). "Human beings" and so-called "animals" occupy the same space(s) and can live in a type of equilibrium if the *linguistic and material conditions of existence* are leveled in favor of a shared terminology of transjection. To put this claim differently, I would say that as we move into the twenty-first century we are returning to a medieval period of thought — a period that is necessarily critical of dyadic distinctions.

Serres writes that

history hides the fact that man is the universal parasite, that everything and everyone around him is a hospitable space. Plants and animals are always his hosts; man is always necessarily their guest. Always taking, never giving. He bends the logic of exchange and of giving in his favor when he is dealing with nature as a whole. When he is dealing with his kind, he continues to do so; he wants to be the parasite of man as well. And his kind want to be so too. Hence rivalry. Hence the sudden, explosive perception of animal humanity, hence the world of animals of the fables.[17]

The "ani-human" exists in her, his, or their own *Umwelt*. The "ani-human" is certainly a parasitical concept, but the concept is also, paradoxically speaking, host-based. Serres insists that "[t]here are some black spots in language,"[18] and these black spots exist because "[w]e are drowning in words and in language. Host is subject, object, friend and enemy."[19] Language presents the symbolic fabric of the ecosystem-site as a means of translation, perception, and communication. Serres points to the importance of conceiving of the parasite as a combinatory and unifying term because the parasite is: "The same at the head,

---

17   Serres, *The Parasite,* 24.
18   Ibid., 16.
19   Ibid., 23.

the other at the tail, or being at the head and nonbeing at the tail, and this middle trunk that is both same and other, being and nonbeing, and so forth."[20] The parasite-body is an Ouroboros of transjection: it eats its tail in a never-ending cycle of eternal recurrence, consumption, mastication, digestion, and rebirth.

In his essay "Vom Nutzen und Nachteil der Historie Für das Leben," Nietzsche situates the parasitic relationship in the following way: "Die Gäste, die zuletzt zur Tafel kommen, sollen mit Recht die letzten Plätze erhalten: und ihr wollt die ersten haben? Nun dann tut wenigstens das Höchste und Größte; vielleicht macht man euch dann wirklich Platz, auch wenn ihr zuletzt kommt."[21] (The guests who come last to the table should in all fairness receive the last places. And you wish to have them first? Then do something of the highest and best order. Perhaps people will then really make a place for you, even if you come at the end [my translation]). The subject who is "allowed" to ignore her or his transjected status does so because of temporal injunctions: those who arrive first conquer first and become *sujets supposé savoir* as "hosts" *par excellence*. This situation leads Serres to insist that

> [h]e [the king] pays for his meal in well turned, well written phrases. And thus he is in the position of the parasite, a universal parasite. One day he will have to understand why the strongest is the parasite — that is to say, the weakest — why the one whose only function is to eat is the one who commands. And speaks. We have just found the place of politics.[22]

Serres considers the undecidable logic of the host and the guest as being mediated, liminal, and transjected as he traces the complexity of power as it travels through the dyad.

---

20 Ibid., 23.
21 Nietzsche, "Vom Nutzen und Nachteil der Historie Für das Leben," 250.
22 Serres, *The Parasite*, 26.

Parasite Sex

Tapeworms are transsexual transjects in that fertilization may occur between two proglottids or within the same proglottid (a proglottid is the term for one of the segments of a tapeworm that contains both male and female sexual organs). The posthuman model of sexuality no longer requires sexed organs of differentiation or social genders of difference because *sameness* has become the model of socio-ontological segmentation. Cloning will be the primary mode of reproduction, Baudrillard argues, as transsexualism becomes the best definition of sexuality.[23] I do not find transsexualism to be the dominant mode of contemporary sexuality, as Baudrillard does, but rather *parasite sexuality*. Parasites contain a proliferation of reproductive organs so that they can impregnate various sections and segments of their own bodies — bodies that function in relation to the interiority of a host. The question of linguistic difference becomes here another unnecessary excess: "him" or "her" is unnecessary for the parasite — a tapeworm, for example, cannot be defined by virtue of sexual or gendered differences. It can also not be defined by traditional ontological differences. A tapeworm is not singular, but a process: it is a life form that lives within its own lifecycle. Deleuze and Guattari are incorrect when they privilege the organ: the *segment* should be the concept that best defines the posthuman model of an assembled-count. Organs do not add up to a totality anymore than segments do. A tapeworm contains a kind of "origin point" in their scolex (or mouth), but this "origin" is only triggered in relation to the host's intestinal wall. The scolex becomes functional only in relation to the codependent love that is triggered between the host-wall and the scolex-parasite. The question becomes then not about sexuality or transsexuality; on the contrary, the question is about love, and more specifically, *codependent love*.

---

23 Jean Baudrillard, *The Perfect Crime,* trans. Chris Turner (London: Verso, 2008), 117.

Parasite sexuality, the kind that occurs within and between segments of the parasite-body, is predicated on the primary love found between parasite and host. Once the love relation is made functional between the host-wall and the scolex, then sex can occur within the parasite. The parasite's "home" is a home of love and the parasite's narcissism becomes paramount as the proglottids reproduce within the host-body. The tapeworm's digestive tract is on its outside: it digests food through its own skin while it touches the host's intestinal wall. The tapeworm is advantageous and opportunistic and models a form of tran-sjected ontology because it exists in between as an un-countable singularity *and* multiplicity. Even though language functions as a virtual parasite, language remains incapable of adequately describing the transjected phorontologies of actual parasites. There are no longer any sex-organs, but only sex-proglottids. The human body is a parasite-body embedded in the abdominal wall of the *Umwelt* or larger ecosystem. The human body feeds alongside the ecology of the world. Every proglottid contains its own independent *dispositifs* or social institutions that act structurally dissimilar from the cosmos of the tapeworm. Insti-tutions are always embedded in a place and feed alongside that place as they are sited within a larger system that parasites the future moment to come. The parasite-body depicts a transject-structure that unsettles binary sign-systems. For this reason, Serres argues that mathematically, "[a] third exists before the second."[24] Even though the structure of language is often bina-ristic, noise is already operative in the informatic relation: the parasite remains in the background, mumbling. The proglottids of the conversation will continually reproduce themselves in an *inter(dis)course* of echoes, murmurs, and mutters.

The parasite is a kind of avant-garde sound poet who adds or multiplies noise in the normative social order. Serres attempts to describe the overall complexity of the parasite when he appears to "throw up his hands" during the following moment of written defeat: "I no longer really know how to say it: the parasite para-

---

24 Serres, *The Parasite*, 63.

sites the parasites. In other words, any given position in the ternary model is, *ad libitum,* parasitic. Who is the third? Someone, anyone. The noise stops; someone leaves. Someone, anyone: both formal and random."[25] Discourse is never fixed when the transjects speak because the transjects only communicate within an inter(dis)course of structural noise. The parasite induces a fractal geography that situates the world — the *Umwelt* — as a system of complexity structured by the communicational nonsense of noise and feedback.

Parasite Hermeneutics: Henry Miller and Conrad Moricand

Henry Miller's *A Devil in Paradise* (1956) features a character notable in literature because this character is the literary emblem of the theoretical parasite. Henry Miller invites a parasitic personality to live with him at his home in Big Sur. The person he invites, Conrad Moricand, is an astrologer by trade who gradually becomes a repugnant character. The "Devil" of Miller's title refers to Moricand, but I think the title is far more evocative (as I will consider momentarily). Serres asks: "The Devil or the Good Lord? Exclusion, inclusion? Thesis or antithesis? The answer is a spectrum, a band, a continuum."[26] A parasite hermeneutics — that I suggest is required to approach a text like *A Devil in Paradise* — would require a Serresian perspective that endorses spectra and continua, sites and para-sites. The "Devil" in Miller's title should be parasited in order to make its opposite simultaneously operative: "A Devil in Paradise" or "A Good Lord in Paradise?" To whom should this transjected spectrum be allocated? Which is Miller? Which is Moricand?

At first, the text is not concerned at all with the question of either the "Devil" or the "Good Lord." Gradually, Moricand is situated and sited as the "Devil." Miller introduces the reader to Moricand by writing that "there was an odor about him,"

---

25 Ibid., 55.
26 Ibid., 57.

which Miller calls, "the aroma of death."[27] When Miller meets Moricand, Moricand has just "begun work on the great theme: Apocatastasis."[28] Apocatastasis is the restitution of the cosmos in which astrological patterns have returned to an earlier state. For Moricand, apocatastasis is a form of recurrence, return, and apology where the sins of the past can be erased to give way to a new tomorrow. However, Moricand is a fatalist by nature, trapped within the dismal conviction of his own inadequacy and melancholy: Miller describes Moricand as "a Stoic dragging his tomb about with him. [...] [T]hough by nature I felt that he was essentially treacherous."[29] Miller "contracts" Moricand from Anaïs Nin who had been infected earlier. Moricand is like an anisaliis tapeworm that is passed from host to host. He had infected Anaïs before Miller and who knows how many others before her: "What Moricand never suspected was that, in presenting him to me, Anaïs hoped to unload some of her burden."[30] Miller, at first, happily accepts the Moricand-infection.

Miller describes, after becoming "burdened" with Moricand, the avidity and voraciousness of Moricand's appetite. Moricand is something that feeds, not only on his host, but also upon a specific site. Moricand's gustatory indulgences do not, however, seem to supply him with any level of nutrition. Moricand does not prosper, but only slowly deteriorates. A phorontological analysis of *A Devil in Paradise* requires that we analyze Miller's parasites as we lay his corpus on the gurney of postmortemism. As 'pataphysical analysts we should cut open Miller's insides and dig around until we can extract the Moricand-worm from Miller's hedonistic intestine. Miller writes that "[n]aturally, from my standpoint, the first and most important thing was to see that the poor devil ate more regularly, and more abundantly. I hadn't the means to guarantee him three meals a day, but I could and did throw a meal into him now and then."[31] Miller's first con-

---

27 Henry Miller, *A Devil in Paradise* (New York: New Directions Bibelot, 1993), 1.
28 Ibid.
29 Ibid., 2.
30 Ibid., 5.
31 Ibid., 5.

cern is to feed his parasite and ensure that the parasite does not starve.

> Sometimes I invited him out to lunch or dinner; more often I invited him to my quarters where I would cook as bountiful and delicious a meal as possible. Half-starved as he was most of the time, it was small wonder that by the end of the meal he was usually drunk. Drunk not with wine, though he drank copiously, but with food, food which his impoverished organism was unable to assimilate in such quantities.[32]

Moricand reaches a jubilant state by consuming an excessive amount of food while being situated as Miller's opposite (or oppo-site): where Miller becomes drunk on water,[33] Moricand becomes drunk on food. Miller and Moricand form the ideal relationship of host and parasite. Food does not sustain or fill Moricand; quite the opposite, the consumption of food seems to require even greater quantities of food: "by the time he had walked home he was hungry all over again."[34] Initially, Miller remains sympathetic to Moricand, but the warning signs of the parasite-infection are present in their preliminary meetings.

Their "friendship" begins when Moricand presents Miller with a copy of Balzac's *Séraphita*.[35] *Séraphita* is a work that can be considered a work of parasite-hermeneutics and transject-literature: Séraphitüs is a transject (an androgyne) who loves Minna (who believes Séraphitüs is a man) and is loved by Wilfrid (who believes Séraphitüs is a woman, Séraphita). This theme of transjection proceeds as Miller and Moricand become trapped within the undecidable relationship of host and parasite.

Moricand is the picture of a parasitic personality who takes advantage of his friends while situating his friends as the only hope: "'The only chance for me at this moment,' he would say

---

32 Ibid., 5–6.
33 Henry Miller, *Sexus: The Rosy Crucifixion: Book One* (New York: Grove Press, 1965), 460.
34 Miller, *A Devil in Paradise,* 6.
35 Ibid., 14.

most solemnly, 'is *you*. There *you* are!' And he would indicate how and where I fitted into the picture."[36] What is the benefit to the parasite? Why does Miller invest so much time and energy into Moricand's survival? Serres argues that the parasite is sometimes productive. Much like Deleuze and Guattari's reterritorialization of desire as productivity, Serres considers parasitism and the infections produced by parasites as creative agents. Against psychoanalytical depictions of desire as lack, Deleuze and Guattari claim that desire is productive, and against medical descriptions of parasitism, Serres situates parasites as creative. According to Serres,

> [t]he parasite invents something new. Since he does not eat like everyone else, he builds a new logic. He crosses the exchange, makes it into a diagonal. He does not barter; he exchanges money. He wants to give his voice for matter, (hot) air for solid, superstructure for infrastructure. People laugh, the parasite is expelled, he is made fun of, he is beaten, he cheats us; but he invents anew."[37]

For Serres, the parasite is engaged in an entirely different gustatory economy than "normal" subjects: the parasite functions within a transject-economy, existing in between stratified lines, eating food that was stolen, borrowed, or exchanged. The parasite is simultaneously a master of rhetoric and also a rhetorical strategy because the parasite is an emblem of rhetoric. Parasitism itself is a rhetorical process because it is a structure that is predicated on the notion of an agenda — an agenda that works in the parasite's best interest and not the host's. This rhetorical economy is situated by Serres within the paradigm of Shannon's information theory: "The parasite invents something new. He obtains energy and pays for it in information. He obtains the roast and pays for it with stories."[38] The parasite is an energetic

---

36 Ibid., 12.
37 Serres, *The Parasite,* 35.
38 Ibid., 36.

catalyzer of systems of knowledge. The parasite joyfully feeds within the hegemonic intestine — surviving and flourishing.

Miller eventually decides to invite Moricand into his home: "Finally I conceived what I thought to be a brilliant idea. Genial, nothing less. It was to invite him to come and live with us, share what we had, regard our home as his own for the rest of his days. It was such a simple solution I wondered why it had never occurred to me before."[39] Moricand gleefully accepts Miller's offer, but before Moricand arrives in America, Miller decides that "[h]e had to be fattened up or I would have an invalid on my hands."[40] To that end, Miller sends Moricand money for food so that when Moricand arrives in America — situating the country as the intestine of plenty — he would already have expanded his appetite on commensal excess.

When Moricand arrives in Big Sur and moves into Miller's home, Miller writes that Moricand "was 'home' at last. Safe, sound, secure."[41] The tapeworm settles into the homey intestinal wall: Moricand's scolex hooks deeply into Miller's psyche. Very rapidly Miller senses "the leech that Anaïs had tried to get rid of. I saw the spoiled child, the man who had never done an honest stroke of work in his life, the destitute individual who was too proud to beg openly but was not above milking a friend dry. I knew it all, felt it all, and already foresaw the end."[42] The importance that Serres affords to the parasite is in its structural relationality: the very idea of relations "is the meaning of the prefix *para-* in the word *parasite*: it is on the side, next to, shifted; it is not on the thing, but on its relation. It has relations, as they say, and makes a system of them."[43] Moricand offers Miller's immune system something to war against. Even though Moricand feeds off of Miller's digestion, Moricand is a mediating character that lives within and alongside the other characters that fill Miller's ecosystem — as his home, peer group, or even America at large.

---

39 Miller, *A Devil in Paradise,* 21.
40 Ibid., 23.
41 Ibid., 25.
42 Ibid., 27.
43 Serres, *The Parasite,* 38–39.

Miller points out that "[i]n one respect he was an ideal house guest — he kept to himself most of the day. Apart from meal times."[44] Meal times lure Moricand from his intestinal cave and to the dinner table. He sits alongside the others, a perfect imitation of a human being, but hungrier than the others and more ravenous because he is not quite "human." Miller's descriptions of Moricand are instructive in this regard because the character remains unfixed and polysemous: "Sometimes he [Moricand] looked Egyptian, sometimes Mongolian, sometimes Iroquois or Mohican, sometimes Chaldean, sometimes Etruscan."[45] Moricand's ethnicity or very physical description is transjected: he is of all cultures and all physicalities. Moricand literally *worms himself* out of any linear or clear description. Miller's description of Moricand renders him monstrous — as something akin to a tapeworm that is the size of a man: "Without a stitch he looks lamentable. Like a broken-down nag. It's not merely that he's potbellied, full of sores and scabs, but that his skin has an unhealthy look, is spotted like tobacco leaf, has no oil, no elasticity, no glow [...]. His flesh seems never to have been in contact with air and sun; it looks half smoked."[46] Moricand's skin is that of a tapeworm because his stomach is on the outside: his skin is not skin. Deleuze and Guattari have no purchase on a character like Moricand because Moricand has no covering-organ of skin; instead, he is covered with the coloring of a proglottid or tape. His body is that of an anisakis.

The room that Moricand lives in is built like a "cell," designed in the same way that a tapeworm furnishes the living arrangements of a colon:

It's true that his cell was tiny, that water leaked through the roof and the windows, that the sow bugs and other bugs took over, that they often dropped on his bed when he was asleep, that to keep warm he had to use an ill-smelling oil stove

---

44 Miller, *A Devil in Paradise,* 30.
45 Ibid., 32–33.
46 Ibid., 95.

which consumed what little oxygen remained after he had sealed up all the cracks and crevices, stuffed the space beneath the door with sacking, shut all the windows tight, and so on […]. And he, poor devil, was cooped up all day, restless, ill at ease, either too hot or too cold, scratching, scratching, and utterly incapable of warding off the hundred and one abominations which materialized out of the ether, for how else explain the presence of all these creeping, crawling, ugly things when all had been shut tight, sealed and fumigated?[47]

Moricand lives alongside other parasites and is similarly parasited. Bed bugs, scabies, lice, and sow bugs have all come to live with the life-size tapeworm. When Moricand goes to see the doctor, the doctor warns Miller about Moricand, saying:

"Do you want my honest advice?"
"I certainly do," said I.
"Then get him off your hands!"
"What do you mean?"
"Just that. You might as well have a leper living with you."
[…]
"It's simple," he said. "He doesn't want to get well. What he wants is sympathy, attention. He's not a man, he's a child. A spoiled child."[48]

Miller takes the doctor's advice to heart and begins to hint to Moricand that he should vacate Miller's home. Moricand tries to weasel out of any commitment to leave in order to maintain his scolex-hold on "paradise": "Once again he agreed, grumblingly, to be sure. Like a rat that had been cornered. But when the time came to depart he was not on hand. He had changed his mind again. What excuse he gave I no longer remember."[49] Eventually, Miller manages to dispose of Moricand, but not before Mori-

---

47 Ibid., 52.
48 Ibid., 54.
49 Ibid., 101.

cand accomplishes one last parasitic act: "Yes, he would con-
sent to accept the passage which had been proffered him, but
on one condition, that I first put to his account in a Paris bank
the equivalent of a thousand dollars."[50] After Miller's housing
of Moricand, this demand is yet another parasitic strategy: the
accomplishment of a con artist and narcissist who does not see
Miller as a friend who has opened up his home, but as a host
who has made his body vulnerable to another organism. Miller calls Moricand "a worm, a leech, a dirty blackmailer,"[51] and
seems to be finally free of him.

However, the parasite in paradise is not only Moricand.
Serres claims that the parasite speaks in parables: "Parabola,
parable, parasite. The parasite pays in parables."[52] Moricand
comes to Miller not only as a parasite, but also as a parable.
The parable in this instance is contained in the *paragram* of the
text and the paragram spells out a name. Serres argues that "the
parable of the parasite and the paralysis of the guest are quite
precisely parallel. [...] [I]t appears in language, in words and
in poems, in parables and paraphrase."[53] The paragram speaks
in the parables of the parasite: language returns to the host as a
para-site. The name of the parasite — the paragram contained in
the parable — is not only "Moricand," but also "Miller." *Paradise*
is itself the mask of a *parasite* because Big Sur is the site of a recurrence. Moricand reflects Miller's own history back to Miller
and *A Devil in Paradise* contains the story of Miller's own apocatastasis. For Miller, apocatastasis is, in this instance, a form of
metastasis that proliferates within the environmental body and
also the physical body. In *Tropic of Cancer* (1934), Miller writes,
regarding his experience of living in France:

I was not only fed... I was feasted. Every night I went
home drunk. [...] I had found a better host; I could afford

50 Ibid., 104.
51 Ibid.
52 Serres, *The Parasite*, 31.
53 Ibid., 32.

to scratch off the ones who were a pain in the ass. But that thought never occurred to them. Finally I had a steady, solid program — a fixed schedule. On Tuesdays I knew it would be this kind of a meal and on Fridays that kind. Cronstadt, I knew, would have champagne for me and homemade apple pie. And Carl would take me out, take me to a different restaurant each time, order rare wines, invite me to the theater afterward or take me to the Cirque Médrano. They were curious about one another, my hosts. Would ask me which place I liked best, who was the best cook, etc.[54]

A Devil in Paradise could easily be re-framed as Cronstadt or Carl's story about feeding Miller during his time in Paris. *A Devil in Paradise* is, from this perspective, the story of a great anxiety: the only difference between Moricand and Miller is that Miller's "charm" has not worn off while Moricand's has. The *better* parasite between the two is Miller: Miller understands that parasitism is intrinsically related to rhetoric. Serres's description of the parasite is akin to a description of Miller's Paris years: "The parasite is invited to the *table d'hôte*; in return, he must regale the other diners with his stories and his mirth. To be exact, he exchanges good talk for good food; he buys his dinner, paying for it in words. It is the oldest profession in the world."[55] Serres's dinner guest/parasite works at Miller and Moricand's true "profession": Miller is arguably more successful than Moricand, but no less parasitic.

Modernism itself, and onwards into the contemporary, is an aesthetic movement that partly celebrates parasitism: from the various fascist-parasites of Eliot, Pound, and Lewis to the emergence of the parasitic antihero, the idea of the modernist patron is structured around the notion that a host-patron pays for the words of a parasite-writer. Both Miller and Joyce famously fed off friends, peers, fellow writers, and patrons. Serres writes that "[h]e [the parasite] is there, well entrenched. Ruins the fa-

---

54 Henry Miller, *Tropic of Cancer* (New York: Grove, 1961), 55.
55 Serres, *The Parasite,* 34.

ther, screws the mother, leads the children, runs the household. We can no longer do without him; he is our system itself: he commands, he has the power, his voice has become that of the master."[56] Serres's description of the parasite here matches the description of a modernist-parasite.

In Eliot's "The Wasteland," for example, the parasite can be found in the repressed rem(a)inder of insurmountable trauma: the parasite is the repression of the memory of the corpse that was planted "last year in your garden"[57] — the soldier's corpse — that acts as the corpse-assemblage of all those killed in the Great War. Modernism is obsessed with figures that feed and exist alongside: the modernist "hero" is an everyman and sometimes a parasite. If Adorno is right when he asserts that to "write poetry after Auschwitz is barbaric,"[58] then there will also be no more aesthetic movements. Poetry and art have become disfigured by a parasite-aesthetics that has taken firm hold with its scolex-grip. There is, in postmortemism, no original, but only the simulated iterations of a form that is fed upon. Towards the end of Joyce's *Ulysses* (1922), Stephen Dedalus and Leopold Bloom encounter Lord John Corley, a character who may well be Conrad Moricand:

The pair parted company and Stephen rejoined Mr Bloom, who, with his practised eye, was not without perceiving that he had succumbed to the blandiloquence of the other parasite. Alluding to the encounter he said, laughingly, Stephen, that is:
— He's down on his luck. He asked me to ask you to ask somebody named Boylan, a billsticker, to give him a job as a sandwichman.[59]

---

56 Ibid., 38.
57 T.S. Eliot, *Collected Poems: 1909–1962* (London: Faber and Faber, 2002), 55.
58 Theodor W. Adorno, *Prisms,* trans. Samuel and Shierry Weber (Cambridge: MIT Press, 1983), 34.
59 James Joyce, *Ulysses* (London: Penguin, 2000), 712.

Corley manages to get half-a-crown out of Stephen and convinces Stephen to ask Bloom if Bloom could ask Blazes Boylan (the man who is sleeping with Bloom's wife, Molly), for a job. *Ulysses* is a text that is predicated on the function of the parasite: if parasites become registered as third parties, as the rupture of noise that disrupts any communicational assemblage, then Joyce's masterpiece proliferates with them. *Ulysses* is an intestine filled to the brim with nematodes and flukes, each of which are replicating. On the one hand, Boylan is a parasite within Bloom's marriage — although Bloom tolerates him because Boylan can function where Bloom cannot. Paradoxically, the affair between Molly and Boylan *strengthens* the marriage between Leopold and Molly because Molly realizes, at the terminus of her soliloquy, that she truly loves Bloom. Boylan is nothing more than a functional vibrator or dildo: a sort of life-size erection.[60] Corley, on the other hand, is a parasite who exchanges half-a-crown for a story and parasitizes Stephen in the process. There are other parasites as well: Stephen is a parasite in the eyes of his dead mother and disappointed father because, instead of writing the "uncreated conscience of [his] race,"[61] Stephen teaches history at a boys' school; and, throughout *Ulysses,* Bloom is racially configured as a parasite living in Ireland — he is seen by other characters as a "Jew" who parasitizes the Irish economy.

Every character in Joyce's Dublin is a third of some other previously "functional" dyad: "The third appears; the third is included. Maybe he is each and every one of us."[62] Other texts in modernism are similarly worried about the parasite or the third: Dorian Gray or Lord Henry in Wilde; Colonel Kurtz in Conrad; Pound's notion of *usura*; or Woolf's Septimus Smith who is considered a psychic and economic drain on society. The parasite

---

60 I wish this were my claim, but it comes from Garry Leonard's appraisal of Boylan as an "erection with an attitude." See Garry Leonard, *Advertising and Commodity Culture in Joyce* (Gainesville: University Press of Florida, 1998), 8.

61 James Joyce, *A Portrait of the Artist as a Young Man* (New York: Signet Classic, 1991), 253.

62 Serres, *The Parasite,* 47.

is a common protagonist or antagonist of modernism and the parasite is now embodied in the conceptual forms of the post-human and the postmortem. The parasite is also the primary figure of a postmortem on the postmodern: the parasite is the entity, homunculus, or author that looks up at us when we cut open the intestinal walls of the postmodern and look backward through time, all the way to the modern and even the Victorian.

The parasite-signal is never *single,* because "[t]he parasite always plugs into the system; the parasite is always there; it is inevitable."[63] Where meaning may have emerged, the parasite proliferates: grinning, twining, and intertwining around sign systems — constrictive and productive. Burroughs reputedly claimed that "[e]very man has inside himself a parasitic being who is acting not at all to his advantage." This "parasitic being" is that part of the self that is metasentient — the component of consciousness that is recursive and self-reflexive. The parasitic being is an imposter that is momentarily embodied: the *Soul* of theology names an entity that is housed inside a body. The soul registers the sins of the body and then must atone for these sins in the afterlife. The soul is akin to a metasentient parasite that has momentarily used the body as a container: if we speculate that the ancient Greek doctrine of metempsychosis is true, then the soul will transmigrate after the death of the body and become a tree, a rock, a wave, an ant, or a bird, etc. However, what if metempsychosis functions in a manner that is more closely related to what Harold Bloom calls the "anxiety of influence?"[64] What if the soul remains a monad that moves across sites and para-sites and parasitizes another body? What if we are floating intelligences that have temporarily infected our hosts and have forgotten about the transition? Metasentience would then be, in this speculative leap, a *realist* code that was transmitted from outer space: it would then be the monolithic residue of a fright-ening anteriority that does not fit into the earthly realm *except*

---

63 Ibid., 63.
64 See Harold Bloom, *The Anxiety of Influence: A Theory of Poetry* (Oxford: Oxford University Press, 1997).

as infection or mutation. In this model, metasentience would be the chance-based fluke that has taken up residence in the *corpus callosum.*

Serres argues that noise functions on the basis of interruption and rupture: "At the first noise, the system is cancelled: if the noise stops, everything comes back to where it was. That shows at least that the parasites are always there, even in the absence of a signal. […] Parasitism is only a linear noise."[65] The Parasite is, for Serres, an interruption or rupture that signals the breakdown of any signal. In phorontological terms, the Parasite is the necessary *clinamen* or swerve that is produced by semantic collisions and that permits the emergence of a communicational system. The noise of the Parasite is what allows the system to instate certain patterns or equilibria. The parasite is therefore truly transjected because it is simultaneously destructive *and* productive: it manifests as a rupture, but this rupture induces stability. Perhaps the Parasite is the name of that undecidable space that exists between the coastline of Britain and the waterline; in other words, the Parasite is one name of the transject, which is, in this case, a nominative paradox that is existent *within* the very structure of language. The Parasite is the gauge that engages language *as* a productive system.

Parasites live everywhere in the world: on the surfaces of kitchen counters, in the soil, within dead bodies, rotten meat, a freshly-sliced piece of sashimi, a pig's eye, or underneath children's fingernails. Pinworm outbreaks occur among children because their immune systems have not yet learned to defend against the limitless array of threats and dangers that fill the *Umwelt.* The Parasite is a structure — as both an actual transject such as a nematode or as a virtual transject such as language — that permits the calibration of meaning within the ecosystem. Derrida argues that "'[d]econstruction' is always attentive to this indestructible logic of parasitism. As a discourse, deconstruction is always a discourse about the parasite, itself a device parasitic on the subject of the parasite, a discourse 'on parasite' and

---

65   Serres, *The Parasite,* 52.

in the logic of the 'superparasite.'"[66] While deconstruction is a discourse that seeks to expose the parasite, it is itself a parasite that provides the parasite the means to remain hidden. Why? Deconstruction is not surgery. Deconstruction does not operate on the levels and architextures that conceal the site. *The parasite lives, first and foremost, within the site.* First, we can deconstruct, but any deconstruction is already the construction of a new site and para-site. However, this problem goes deeper still: the parasite of language is akin to a self-replicating meme that rebuilds itself as quickly as any discourse can deconstruct it. The primary problem of the parasite is that there is no way to kill it off. This problem arises because any speculative definition of ontology — in postmortemism — can no longer be about Being *qua* Being; on the contrary, any definition of ontology should be phorontological: ontology today should not deconstruct, but *operate* on the postmortem. Such a postmortem practice would focus on *Being quartered beings* instead of Being *qua* Being. The first question asked by phorontology is: *what counting system is being privileged*? The second question is then: *how can we locate the o and the 1*? From within the zero and the One, the parasite emerges as the third that was waiting within the binary prior to the birth of any supposed anthropocentric subject.

Language Parasites does not express a metaphysical infection akin to Morgellons Disease. Morgellons is, according to allopathic medicine, an instance of delusional parasitosis in which a patient believes that she or he is infected with a variety of parasites. There are similarities between my project and Morgellons though because I am describing a *linguistic parasitosis*. Jean-Louis Gault writes that

[t]he only illness we suffer from as speaking beings is the one introduced into the living by the parasitism of the signifier. Lacan spoke of language as a cancer and evoked the viru-

---

66 Jacques Derrida, "The Rhetoric of Drugs," trans. Michael Israel, in *High Culture: Reflections on Addiction and Modernity*, eds. Anna Alexander and Mark S. Roberts, 19–43 (Albany: SUNY Press, 2003), 24.

lence of *logos*. He defined the unconscious as the effects of speech on the subject, and he showed that the Freudian clinic developed the incidences of the illness of the signifier.[67]

The signifier produces illness and infection within the subject and, for this reason, the signifier is one of the names of the Parasite. If phorontology is a method of operation on the ill subject — an approach that begins surgery with a de-scission — then the Parasite becomes an entity that is operated upon; an entity that, when removed, can locate the site. This so-called "site" is not originary though because it is only ever a 'patasite, which is a site that is beyond metaphysics — an absurd space of infinite de-scissions where the cutting never terminates in a final cut. The 'patasite is a place of exhaustion where the surgeon momentarily rests, dripping sweat into the corpus of the patient who waits with the ennui of a dead reader. The Decision reached by a de-scission is only ever a *desiting* because any desiting immediately inscribes — materially and semiotically — a new site and this "new site" should be termed a 'patasite due to the manner in which a 'patasite remains absurd until its contingencies and exigencies have been located. Any teleology of this newly discovered 'patasite would progress through four ontological stages: 1) the materiality of the site, 2) the potentiality of the implied parasite, 3) the virtuality of the metasite that remains beyond the triadic relation of site-parasite-site, and 4) the resultant 'patasite that registers a true form of far-from-equilibrium complexity. The 'patasite is placed at a place that is beyond any beyond: it is a theoretically capacious realm that is occupied by heretofore-unknown subjective entities that I call *xenojects*. Such alien identities are so inconceivably other from anthropocentric epistemologies or philosophies that they must be considered apart from and alongside already sited notions of exteriority.

---

67 Jean-Louis Gault, "Two Statuses of the Symptom: 'Let Us Turn to Finn Again,'" in *The Later Lacan: An Introduction,* eds. Véronique Voruz and Bogdan Wolf (Albany: SUNY Press, 2007), 73–82, 79.

Phorontology would be the best analytic approach for considering the xenoject. Assuming that the human species escapes Earth when our sun becomes a red giant and engulfs the first two or three planets of our solar system, then various other lives and subjects will become actualized as water thaws on Jupiter's moons. The xenoject is an alien subjectivity that requires theorization in order to understand Being in all of its permutations — every possible human, posthuman, inhuman, and nonhuman manifestation or variety. An appropriate contemporary theory of Being should encompass not only every marginalized being or identity held at the limits of phenomenology, but also every other possible configuration of Being that may exist or *potentially exist* within our solar system, galaxy, and universe: the general name of this "being" is "xenoject."

Returning to the earthly realm, the parasite is psychically a *parapsyche* that has been transjected, thereby unsettling the possibility of anything ever being indivisible. The very term *individual* was originally meant to describe the same state as the atomic: a state of indivisibility. The atom and the individual are epistemological constructs that were originally defined as being unsplittable; hence, these concepts are countable, singular, and seemingly agential. The problem here is raised by the parasite: both the atom and the individual are constructs of a language that is structured as a parasite-system and yet both are, in realist terms, splittable entities. The atom can be split into countless particularities and the individual can be dismembered like a carceral body strung up on Foucault's scaffold. The individual is, I claim, in the contemporary transjected era, the *dividual*. The individual is a concept that functions *against* division whereas what I call the "dividual" pertains to particulate social orders and the dismembered corpus of the individual. The individual is, quite literally, *dual* or multiple. The duality present within the individual is localized in the figure of the parasite or the third party that permits the imaginary coherence of the dyadic structure (site–site) to remain "whole." The parasite is therefore the hyphen (or noise) that exists between any two sites, be they self–other, good–evil, or individual–institution. A dividual is then the proper, realist name of the subject within the contemporary social realm. The individual is a member of the social and, as a member, lives with the possibility of being *dismembered* (as a dividual) or *remembered* at a future site-to-come. Where the individual forgets, the dividual remembers.

The parasite is a *res*-of-chaos — a chaotic thing — that structures ontology as a phorontology and renders the world as an imaginary unity that features indiscernible patterns amidst universal entropy and undeniable chaos. The parasite names the fractal shape of the dividual, the de-scission, and the sites that structure the inhabited world.

Exergum: Transject Manifesto

We are the new workers of phenomenology.

Our being is our labor.

We no longer *be* in any manner that delimits the self to a binary, boundary, dyad, or decision.

We work in the tradition of Husserl, Heidegger, and Merleau-Ponty, but do not remain contained in a hegemonic paradigm of masculine, heteronormative, white, or able-bodied perspectives. This older subject is the dead corpse of the author on the gurney of textuality.

Grounds:

A *ject* is thrown: the thrownness of *jection* appears as either an interjection or an introjection — this process situates projects, dejects, and rejects within various cages, jail cells, government buildings, and draconian facades of Kantian schemata.

Every schemata is a building and every building is built upon a site that requires excavation.

The age-old subject and object binary is unnecessary, duplicitous, discursive — a delimiting jail cell of constraint. We must break the Lacanian *barres* of our schematized prison(s).

Transjection:

The transject (like the subject, the object, the deject, and the project) is a field-specific and local name of an ontological entity.

The "subject" has been the appropriate name for the ontological entity also known as a "human being" because of specific historical and ideological dictates. We are, traditionally speaking, subjects: *subjects of* a king, *subjects of* a state, *subjects of* an institutionalized power structure. We have been subjected. Endlessly. The revolution must, at its core, resist any ontologization of the self as "subject."

We are now subject-ofs, which are the small micro identities that inhabit a transject.

Every "of" is a parasite that feeds upon your identity and, conversely, renders that identity as only ever imaginarily coherent.

The transject has become a terminological necessity in our contemporary era. The transject describes what is really happening *on the street,* outside of the ivory tower.

However, even inside the ivory tower contemporary philosophy has reflected the emergence of this new category in its concern with liminal categories: philosophers now ask (and have been asking for several decades), "how can we think the in between?"

The transject is the name of an ontological category that is represented by realist instances of parasites and expands to include many other liminal states of being.

Is the liminal doubly parasitic then? Parasitic to both sides? Does one side — and what are these sides or borders? — get jealous of the other? A bifurcated, disloyal, and polygamous parasite is worse than one who steals the entire life force of the border entities. To share one's parasite is the great melancholic crisis of the border state: it is the true reason why liminality is disparaged, feared, policed, sought out, and, fundamentally, destroyed.

The Xenoject:

The secret ontological name of all that exists is "xenoject." The xenoject is the generic category of every possible ontological state that may exist in our own solar system, galaxy, universe, and every other possible dimensional variant.

If your self exists as another self in another universe or another poly-dimensional brane, then that self is *xenojected* as a component of your self that exists elsewhere.

Every "subject" is only a small, localized category of an overall unthinkable xenoject.

The human sciences and humanities have developed to the point where we can finally begin to consider the xenoject.

The xenoject encompasses imagined selves, various identities, and even dream states of self.

The xenoject even encompasses a vitalist understanding of ontology where every rock, or twig, or branch, or creature, or temporarily unified entity contains an energetic piece of self.

The xenoject encompasses any of the "souls" you may have had or may have, including every metempsychotic iteration of your own self and every other alien self. (Perhaps part of your xenoject lives in another brane, in another galaxy, as an amoeba in an alien ocean).

Outsides of the Outside:

We can now begin to think about the phenomenologically anterior.

The "xenoject" and the "transject" are expressions of a postmortem era in which textuality has become something much weirder, nonlinear, and aperiodic than ever before. Now texts are as material as the bodies they inscribe and the bodies they inscribe are as incorporeal as Communion wafers.

We have entered the postmortem of the postmodern.

All our corpses wait on the gurney of our transjections.

Bibliography

Adorno, Theodor W. *Prisms.* Translated by Samuel and Shierry Weber. Cambridge: MIT Press, 1983.

Agamben, Giorgio. *Homo Sacer: Sovereign Power and Bare Life.* Translated by Daniel Heller-Roazen. Palo Alto: Stanford University Press, 1998.

———. *What is an Apparatus? And Other Essays.* Stanford: Stanford University Press, 2009.

Althusser, Louis. *On Ideology.* Translated by Ben Brewster. London: Verso, 2008.

Austin, J.L., *How to Do Things with Words.* Cambridge: Harvard University Press, 1962.

Baudrillard, Jean. *The Perfect Crime.* Translated by Chris Turner. London: Verso, 2008.

———. *Simulacra and Simulation.* Translated by Sheila Faria Glaser. Ann Arbor: University of Michigan Press, 1994.

Bell, Shannon. *Fast Feminism.* New York: Autonomedia, 2010.

Berglund, Jeff. *Cannibal Fictions: American Explorations of Colonialism, Race, Gender, and Sexuality.* Madison: the University of Wisconsin Press, 2006.

Bergvall, Caroline. *Meddle English: New and Selected Texts.* Callicoon: Nightboat Books, 2011.

Birkerts, Sven. *The Gutenberg Elegies: The Fate of Reading in an Electronic Age.* New York: Farrar, Straus and Giroux, 2006.

Bloom, Harold. *The Anxiety of Influence: A Theory of Poetry.* Oxford: Oxford University Press, 1997.

Bök, Christian. *The Xenotext: Book 1.* Toronto: Coach House, 2015.

———. "The Xenotext Experiment," *SCRIPTed* 5 (2008): 228–31.

Brassier, Ray. *Nihil Unbound: Enlightenment and Extinction* (London: Palgrave Macmillan, 2007)

Braune, Sean. "Cage's Mesostics and Saussure's Paragrams as Love Letters," *Postmodern Culture* 22, no. 2 (2012): n.p.

Burroughs, William S. *The Ticket That Exploded.* New York: Grove, 1992.

———— and Brion Gysin. *The Exterminator.* San Francisco: Dave Haselwood Books, 1967.

Chomsky, Noam. "Authors@Google: Noam Chomsky," April 25, 2008, http://www.youtube.com/watch?v=rnLWSC5p1XE.

————. *Language and Mind.* Cambridge: Cambridge University Press, 2006.

Condliffe, Jamie. "Cryptic Poetry Written in a Microbe's DNA," *NewScientist,* May 4, 2011, https://www.newscientist.com/blogs/culturelab/2011/05/christian-boks-dynamic-dna-poetry.html.

Dawkins, Richard. *The Selfish Gene.* Oxford: Oxford University Press, 2006.

Derrida, Jacques. *Limited Inc.* Translated by Jeffrey Mehlman. Evanston: Northwestern University Press, 1988.

————. *Of Grammatology: Corrected Edition.* Translated by Gayatri Chakravorty Spivak. Baltimore: Johns Hopkins University Press, 1997.

————. "The Rhetoric of Drugs," trans. Michael Israel. In *High Culture: Reflections on Addiction and Modernity,* eds. Anna Alexander and Mark S. Roberts. Albany: SUNY Press, 2003), 19–43.

Dewdney, Christopher. *The Immaculate Perception.* Toronto: Anansi, 1986.

————. "Parasite Maintenance." In *Alter Sublime,* 75–92. Toronto: Coach House, 1980.

Dworkin, Andrea. *Intercourse.* New York: Basic Books, 2007.

Eliot, T.S. *Collected Poems: 1909–1962.* London: Faber and Faber, 2002.

Foucault, Michel. "Of Other Spaces," trans. Jay Miskowiec. *Diacritics* 16, no. 1 (1986): 22–27.

Fukuyama, Francis. *The End of History and the Last Man.* New York: Free Press, 2006.

Gault, Jean-Louis. "Two Statuses of the Symptom: 'Let Us Turn to Finn Again.'" In *The Later Lacan: An Introduction,* eds. Véronique Voruz and Bogdan Wolf, 73–82 Albany: SUNY Press, 2007.

Goldsmith, Kenneth. *Traffic.* Los Angeles: Make Now Press, 2007.

———. *The Weather.* Los Angeles: Make Now Press, 2005.

Heidegger, Martin. *Being and Time.* Translated by John Macquarrie and Edward Robinson. New York: HarperPerennial, 2008.

———. "Letter on Humanism." In *Basic Writings,* trans. Frank A. Capuzzi in collaboration with J. Glenn Gray, 213–66. New York: HarperCollins, 1993).

———. *Unterwegs zur Sprache.* Frankfurt am Main: Vittorio Klostermann, 1985.

Innis, Harold A. *Empire and Communications.* Toronto: Dundurn, 2007.

Jakobson, Roman. "Closing Statement: Linguistics and Poetics." In *Style in Language,* ed. Thomas Sebeok, 350–77. Cambridge: MIT Press, 1960.

Jameson, Fredric. *Postmodernism: or, The Cultural Logic of Late Capitalism.* Durham: Duke University Press, 2005.

———. *The Political Unconscious: Narrative as a Socially Symbolic Act.* Ithaca: Cornell University Press, 1982.

Jarry, Alfred. *Exploits & Opinions of Dr. Faustroll, Pataphysician.* Translated by Simon Watson Taylor. Boston: Exact Change, 1996.

Joyce, James. *A Portrait of the Artist as a Young Man.* New York: Signet Classic, 1991.

———. *Ulysses.* London: Penguin, 2000.

Lacan, Jacques. *Écrits: The First Complete Edition in English.* Translated by Bruce Fink, with Héloïse Fink and Russell Grigg. New York: Norton, 2006.

———. *The Seminar of Jacques Lacan: Book III: The Psychoses 1955–1956.* Edited by Jacques-Alain Miller and translated by Russell Grigg. New York: Norton, 1997.

———. *The Seminar of Jacques Lacan: Book XVII: The Other Side of Psychoanalysis.* Edited by Jacques-Alain Miller and translated by Russell Grigg. New York: Norton, 2007.

———. *The Seminar of Jacques Lacan: On Feminine Sexuality, The Limits of Love and Knowledge: Book XX: Encore 1972–1973.* Edited by Jacques-Alain Miller and translated by Bruce Fink. New York: Norton, 1999.

Leonard, Garry. *Advertising and Commodity Culture in Joyce.* Gainesville: University Press of Florida, 1998.

Lucretius. *On the Nature of Things: De rerum natura.* Edited and translated by Anthony M. Esolen. Baltimore: The Johns Hopkins University Press, 1995.

Mandelbrot, Benoit B. *The Fractal Geometry of Nature.* New York: W.H. Freeman and Company, 2000.

Mullarkey, John, and Anthony Paul Smith. "Introduction: The Non-Philosophical Inversion: Laruelle's Knowledge Without Domination." In *Laruelle and Non-Philosophy,* eds. John Mullarkey and Anthony Paul Smith, 1–18. Edinburgh: Edinburgh University Press, 2012.

Marra, Michael F. "Things and Words." In *Japan's Frames of Meaning: A Hermeneutics Reader,* ed. Michael F. Marra, 3–50. Honolulu: University of Hawai'i Press, 2011.

Margulis, Lynn, and Dorion Sagan. *Microcosmos: Four Billion Years of Evolution from Our Microbial Ancestors.* Berkeley: University of California Press, 1997.

Marx, Karl. *Selected Writings.* Edited by David McLellan. Oxford: Oxford University Press, 2007.

McCaffery, Steve. *Prior to Meaning: The Protosemantic and Poetics.* Evanston: Northwestern University Press, 2001.

McLuhan, Marshall. *The Gutenberg Galaxy: The Making of Typographic Man.* Toronto: University of Toronto Press, 2002.

Melgard, Holly. *The Making of Americans.* Troll Thread Press, 2012.

Miller, Henry. *A Devil in Paradise.* New York: New Directions Bibelot, 1993.

――――. *Sexus: The Rosy Crucifixion: Book One.* New York: Grove Press, 1965.

――――. *Tropic of Cancer.* New York: Grove, 1961.

Niebisch, Arndt. *Media Parasites in the Early Avant-Garde: On the Abuse of Technology and Communication.* New York: Palgrave Macmillan, 2012.

Nietzsche, Friedrich. "On Truth and Lies in a Nonmoral Sense," In *Philosophy and Truth: Selections from Nietzsche's Note-Books of the Early 1870s,* ed. and trans. Daniel Breazeale. New Jersey: Humanities Press, 1979.

――――. "Vom Nutzen und Nachteil der Historie Für das Leben." In *Werke in Drei Bänden: Erster Band,* 209–85. Munich: Carl Hanser Verlag, 1954.

Ong, Walter J. *Orality and Literacy: The Technologizing of the Word.* London: Routledge, 2002.

Parikka, Jussi. *Insect Media: An Archaeology of Animals and Technology.* Minneapolis: University of Minnesota Press, 2010.

Prigogine, Ilya, and Isabelle Stengers. "Postface: Dynamics from Leibniz to Lucretius." In Michel Serres, *Hermes: Literature, Science, Philosophy,* eds. Josué V. Harari and David F. Bell, 135–55. Baltimore: Johns Hopkins University Press, 1982.

Ricoeur, Paul. *The Rule of Metaphor: The Creation of Meaning in Language.* Translated by Robert Czerny with Kathleen McLaughlin and John Costello, SJ. London: Routledge, 2003.

Roudinesco, Elisabeth. *Jacques Lacan: An Outline of a Life and a History of a System of Thought.* Translated by Barbara Bray. Cambridge: Polity, 2005.

Schutt, Bill. *Cannibalism: A Perfectly Natural History.* Chapel Hill: Algonquin Books, 2017.

Sebeok, Thomas A. *Perspectives in Zoosemiotics.* The Hague: Mouton de Gruyter, 1972.

Serres, Michel. *The Parasite.* Translated by Lawrence R. Schehr. Minneapolis: University of Minnesota Press, 2007.

*sh*Cherbak, Vladimir I., and Maxim A. Makukov. "The 'Wow! signal' of the terrestrial genetic code," accepted for publication in *Icarus,* arXiv: 1303.6739v1 (Sub. 2013, March 27).

Shillingsburg, Peter L. *From Gutenberg to Google: Electronic Representations of Literary Texts.* Cambridge: Cambridge University Press, 2006.

Shipley, Gary J. *The Death of Conrad Unger: Some Conjectures Regarding Parasitosis and Associated Suicide Behavior.* Brooklyn: Punctum Books, 2012.

Starobinski, Jean. *Words upon Words: The Anagrams of Ferdinand de Saussure.* Translated by Olivia Emmet. New Haven: Yale University Press, 1979.

Stein, Gertrude. *The Making of Americans: Being a History of a Family's Progress.* London: Dalkey Archive, 2006.

Waldman, Dan. "Monkey Apes Humans by Walking on Two Legs," *NBCnews.com,* July 21, 2004, http://www.nbcnews.com/id/5479501#.UxehNXmN1G4.

Watts, Peter. "Brain Damage. The Very Essence of Humanity," *Rifters,* July 22, 2004, http://www.rifters.com/real/newscrawl_2004.htm.

———. "The Secret of Sentience," *Rifters,* August 6, 2004, http://www.rifters.com/real/newscrawl_2004.htm.

Wershler-Henry, Darren. *the tapeworm foundry: andor the dangerous prevalence of imagination.* Toronto: Anansi, 2000.

Wheeler, William Morton. "The Ant-Colony as an Organism," *The Journal of Morphology* 22, no. 2 (1911): 307–25.

———. *The Social Insects, Their Origin and Evolution.* New York: Harcourt Brace, 1928.

Williams, Alex, and Nick Srnicek. "#Accelerate: Manifesto for an Accelerationist Politics," *#ACCELERATE: The Accelerationist Reader,* 347–62. Falmouth: Urbanomic, 2014.

Žižek, Slavoj. *Enjoy Your Symptom!: Jacques Lacan in Hollywood and Out.* New York: Routledge, 2008.

———. *The Sublime Object of Ideology.* London: Verso, 1989.

Index of Names and Concepts

64796342R00078

Made in the USA
San Bernardino, CA
23 December 2017